POLISH WINGS 35

Wojtek Matusiak

Supermarine Spitfire V
Polish Squadrons over Dieppe

CHALK UP
A
VICTORY

● You are tempted to buy something. Do you really need it? NO—so you don't buy, and chalk up a victory for yourself. The money you save by each victory can be lent to your country. It is needed to help give our airmen more and more machines.

WAR SAVINGS
will bring WINGS FOR VICTORY

W.F.L. 97. Issued by the National Savings Committee, London; the Scottish Savings Committee, Edinburgh; the Ulster Savings Committee, Belfast.

STRATUS

Polish Wings

Wydawnictwo STRATUS s.j.
ul. Żeromskiego 4, 27-600 Sandomierz 1, Poland
e-mail: office@stratusbooks.pl
www.stratusbooks.com.pl
www.mmpbooks.biz
Copyright © 2022 Stratus,
Copyright © 2022 Wojtek Matusiak

ISBN 978-83-67227-01-8

Layout concept	Bartłomiej Belcarz
Cover concept	Artur Juszczak
Cover	Marek Ryś
Proofreading	Roger Wallsgrove
DTP	Wojtek Matusiak
	Stratus sp.j.
Colour Drawings	Robert Grudzień

PRINTED IN POLAND

Photograph credits:
Arct family, Peter R. Arnold, Krzysztof Barbarski, Bartłomiej Belcarz, Steve Brooking, Jim Brzózkiewicz, Carol Gradwell, Łukasz Gredys, Robert Gretzyngier, Tony Holmes, Adam Jackowski, Jakubowski family, Adam Jarski, Michał Jaroszyński-Wolfram, Benedict Jan Kolczyński, Kołaczkowski family, Tomasz Kopański, Wojciech Krajewski, Tadeusz Królikiewicz, Zbigniew Legierski, Wojtek Matusiak, Mike Melaney, Wilhelm Ratuszyński, Daniel Rolski, Wojciech Sankowski, Piotr Sikora, Grzegorz Sojda, Grzegorz Śliżewski, Helmut Terbeck, Paweł Tuliński, Wandzilak family, Wojda family, Waldemar Wójcik, Wyszkowski family, Józef Zieliński, Wojciech Zmyślony, Battle of Britain Bunker – Uxbridge, Fleet Air Arm Museum – Yeovilton, Imperial War Museum - London, Muzeum Lotnictwa Polskiego – Cracow, Muzeum Wojska Polskiego – Warsaw, Polish Air Force Memorial Committee – Northolt, Polish Institute and Sikorski Museum – London, Royal Air Force Museum – Hendon.

My special thanks to Bob Sikkel for his invaluable assistance (which actually started well before I commenced work on this book, when he recommended David O'Keefe's 'One Day in August' to me). Wojciech Zmyślony (www.polishairforce.pl) once more provided many valuable comments and suggestions. Robert Grudzień's input was, again, much more than just the colour plates.

Wojtek Matusiak

Previous page: A well known propaganda photo of S/Ldr Jan Zumbach in the cockpit of his Spitfire VB EP594 RF-D, taken not long after 'Jubilee'. The scoreboard includes his victories claimed during the operation. The image was used in a 'Wings for Victory' War Savings leaflet issued jointly by the British savings committees in London, Edinburgh and Belfast.

Front and back covers: Spitfire VB AB183 RF-A from No. 303 Squadron during Operation 'Jubilee', 19 August 1942.

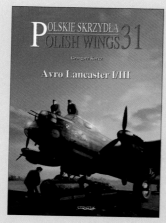

SUPERMARINE SPITFIRE V
Polish Squadrons over Dieppe

This book is a tribute to Fighter Command's most successful wing during operation 'Jubilee'. Several hundred carefully selected and extensively captioned images depict Spitfires of the 1st Polish Wing, and the men who maintained and flew them in support of the Dieppe landings.

The assault of Allied (mostly Canadian) troops at Dieppe on Wednesday, 19 August 1942, has been one of the most controversial battles of the Second World War. Its aims are claimed to have been (in no particular order): to obtain experience of landing a major military force on enemy held coast in order to help prepare proper invasion(s) for the future; to obtain vital intelligence from enemy headquarters captured during the raid in order to help in other aspects of the war, particularly the Battle of the Atlantic; to demonstrate the willingness of the Western Allies to conduct war in Europe by all available means in order to strengthen the Soviet resistance against the Germans; to demonstrate the ability of the Western Allies to mount a successful landing on the French coast in order to divert German forces from other theatres of the war; to demonstrate that full-scale invasion in France was not (yet) possible and the campaign in North Africa should take precedence.

The military and political background of the operation, and details of the military actions on the ground, at sea and in the air, are beyond the scope of this book. The essentials of the landings as provided at the time to the military personnel are reprinted in Appendix I on p. 85. More details can be found in numerous publications on the subject. This author's favourite is David O'Keefe's 'One Day in August. The Untold Story behind Canada's Tragedy at Dieppe'.

The aim of the air operations associated with 'Jubilee' was to provide direct support to the amphibious landing and to defend the troops and the fleet against the *Luftwaffe*. Again, the official military narrative of the time is reprinted in Appendix I. A detailed description can be found in the fundamental book 'The Greatest Air Battle. Dieppe, 19th August 1942' by Norman Franks, which is strongly recommended.

It is noteworthy that the air battle over Dieppe on 19 August 1942 was fought by a truly cosmopolitan community. Of the 48 Spitfire squadrons, only half were British units of the RAF. The other 24 included six manned by Canadians, five by Poles, two each by Czechoslovaks and Norwegians, one each by Belgians, 'Free French' and New Zealanders. Notably, there were altogether six US-manned Spitfire squadrons: three of these being the RAF 'Eagle Squadrons' and the other three forming the 31st Fighter Group USAAF. 'Jubilee' was the very first occasion when US 'star-spangled' fighters engaged the *Luftwaffe*, and these USAAF fighters were Spitfires, because the Americans had no equal single-engined fighters of their own design at the time.

[1]: Dieppe harbour in 1942.

1st Polish Wing in mid-1942

In mid-1942 the 1st Polish Wing (Fighter Command's Northolt Wing) was the primary fighter force of the exiled Polish Air Force. It was headquartered at RAF Northolt, which was also the base of two of its squadrons, Nos. 306 and 317, as of late June 1942. The other two squadrons, Nos. 302 and 316 at the time, were based at RAF Heston, used as a satellite aerodrome by the 1st Wing.

The other three Polish fighter squadrons (Nos. 303, 308 and 315 in late June 1942) were based in the North of England. They formed the 2nd Polish Wing, whose main role was operational training and providing replacement pilots for the 1st Wing. To ensure even combat effort distribution among all Polish squadrons, they rotated between the two wings. At the end of July 1942 No. 308 Sqn moved south to join the 1st Wing, replacing No. 316 which transferred north for a period of rest.

The Fighter Command plans for the Dieppe landings, both in June for 'Rutter' and in August for 'Jubilee', called for reinforcement of the 1st Wing by one of the squadrons of the 2nd Wing (No. 308 in June and No. 303 in August).

Throughout the summer of 1942 the 1st Polish Wing was led by W/Cdr Stefan Janus and his deputy S/Ldr Tadeusz Nowierski. Notably, the exiled Polish Air Force was not part of the RAF (as is commonly, and incorrectly, assumed), and the scope of duty of the officer commanding a Polish wing was significantly broader than that of an RAF Wing Leader. The latter was a deputy of an RAF Station Commander, and his duty was to plan and command operations by the fighter squadrons of the wing. For a commander of a Polish wing this was just part of his duties, however. Because of Polish AF legal independence from the RAF, he also dealt with various administrative and disciplinary actions related to the existence of the wing that would not bother an RAF Wing Leader.

For more information on the Polish Spitfire V squadrons, their aircraft and operations, see the 'Supermarine Spitfire V' vols. 1 and 2 ('Polish Wings' series nos. 29 and 30) by this author.

[2]: W/Cdr Stefan Janus, commanding the 1st Polish Wing at Northolt, (left) in discussion with S/Ldr Stanisław Skalski, commanding No. 317 Sqn (right) and F/Lt Zygmunt Bieńkowski, No. 303 Sqn 'A' Flight Commander, photographed in July 1942 in the south-western dispersal (used by No. 317 Sqn at the time) at Northolt. No. 303 was part of the 2nd Wing at the time.

[3]: Another photo taken at the same location and about the same time. Left to right: S/Ldr Skalski, G/Cpt Alfred Guy Adnams (RAF Northolt Station Commander) and W/Cdr Tadeusz Henryk Rolski. Rolski was the senior Polish Operations Officer at HQ No. 11 Group at Uxbridge at the time, and a frequent visitor to Northolt, where he had earlier commanded the 1st Wing between mid-1941 and early 1942.

[4]: S/Ldr Tadeusz Nowierski was the deputy of W/Cdr Janus at Northolt.

[5]: W/Cdr Stefan Witorzeńć, commanding the 2nd Polish Wing at Kirton-in-Lindsey. The 2nd Polish Wing at the time was where squadrons rested after a period of intensive flying over the Continent. Both at the time of 'Rutter' and then 'Jubilee' one of its squadrons was deployed down south to join the 1st Wing during the operation. W/Cdr Witorzeńć himself did not fly operationally in 'Jubilee', however.

Operation 'Rutter'

When discussing the Dieppe landings, the interest is, naturally, focused on 19 August 1942 and operation 'Jubilee'. However, the first plan of a landing at Dieppe was code-named 'Rutter' and scheduled to take place in June or July 1942. From the outset, it was planned as a one-day operation ending in withdrawal of the troops back to Britain.

To achieve Allied air supremacy over the landing zone, a large fighter force was concentrated in southern England for the duration of the operation. Among others, the 1st Polish Wing squadrons moved temporarily to Croydon (Nos. 306 & 317 from Northolt and Nos. 302 & 316 from Heston). Additionally, No. 308 (at the time part of the 2nd Wing) moved to Redhill. In the words of the June 1942 summary in the Combat Diary of RAF Northolt: 'This move was originally timed for 16/6/42 but was postponed until 30/6/42. Croydon was a bad aerodrome for a Spitfire Wing and three aircraft were crashed on landing.' The landing accidents on deployment from Northolt were suffered by No. 306 Sqn pilots F/O Władysław Walendowski in Spitfire VB BM568 UZ-H and Sgt Wawrzyniec Jasiński in AA847 UZ-V (both aircraft repairable on site), and also by F/O Zbigniew Janicki from No. 317 Sqn in W3970 JH-Y (the Spitfire had to be sent away for repairs).

The July 1942 summary of the same document said: 'The first seven days of this month were spent waiting for combined operations against Dieppe to take place. The weather broke up before suitable conditions were obtained and Squadrons returned to their normal bases.'

'Rutter' failed to materialise, but it cost the Polish squadrons more casualties. On 3 July No. 302 Sqn's BL990 WX-K was seriously damaged in a landing accident at Croydon when flown by P/O Jerzy Paczuski. Two days later, on the 5th, P/O Marian Kotlarz in BL525 ZF-J started a very bad series for No. 308 Sqn at Redhill, when he damaged his flaps in a take-off collision with a stationary aircraft and then overshot on landing due to flap unserviceability. The aircraft had to be sent away for repairs, but the pilot was unhurt. 6 July was a tragic day: Sgt Witold Herbst in BL482 (code unknown) collided with P/O Julian Kawczyński in BL624 ZF-X. The latter was killed, while Herbst survived, badly injured. The next day saw the final act of the bad series for No. 308 Sqn, when F/O Józef Sobolewski belly-landed BL473 at Redhill. He was unhurt, but the Spitfire had

to be sent away to be repaired. It was also on 7 July that Sgt Piotr Kuryłowicz from No. 317 Sqn suffered a landing accident at Northolt in EN919 JH-N upon return from Croydon.

Altogether, the operation that did not happen cost the five Polish squadrons one pilot killed and one seriously injured, two Spitfires destroyed and seven seriously damaged. This did not differ much from the casualties during 'Jubilee', in the face of the enemy: one pilot killed and one PoW, three Spitfires destroyed and five seriously damaged!

Before 'Rutter' was cancelled, special markings were applied in the first days of July 1942 on fighters assembled for it: white bands on top of the nose and tailplane. These were removed after a few days. Notably, no special markings were used during operation 'Jubilee', even though the legend that the white nose bands were applied for the August Dieppe landings persists to date.

The purpose of these markings in July remains obscure. Applied on the top surfaces, they could serve little purpose in helping the navy and the army in the identification of friendly aircraft. One hypothesis is that these bands were part of Allied intelligence decoy operations, intended to make Hitler believe a real invasion of France was forthcoming. Such markings, conspicuous from above, could be spotted by *Luftwaffe* aerial reconnaissance and help persuade the Germans that some major operation was afoot. It is a fact that about that time, at the height of the German offensive towards Stalingrad, Hitler did withdraw troops from Russia to France for defence against possible Allied landings.

[6]: Senior officers of the Polish fighter force at RAF Croydon on 5 July 1942. Left to right: S/Ldr Walerian Żak (commanding No. 308 Sqn, detached from the 2nd Polish Wing to the 1st Wing for operation 'Rutter'), W/Cdr Stefan Witorzeń, G/Cpt Stefan Pawlikowski (Senior Polish Liaison Officer to HQ Fighter Command, i.e. commanding the Polish fighter force in Britain), W/Cdr Stefan Janus and S/Ldr Witold Urbanowicz (on attachment to the 1st Polish Wing at the time).

[7]: Close-up photo of, left to right: W/Cdr Stefan Janus, S/Ldr Witold Urbanowicz and G/Cpt Stefan Pawlikowski. Pawlikowski (born in 1896), whose fighter pilot's career started in WW1, would be the oldest pilot to fly on operations during 'Jubilee'.

[8–9]: No. 302 Squadron dispersal at RAF Croydon in June 1942.

[10]: No. 306 Sqn pilots in front of the Officers' Mess at RAF Croydon in June 1942. Left to right: P/O Jerzy Polak, P/O Henryk Pietrzak, F/O Antoni Krąkowski, F/Lt Józef Gil and P/O Roman Pentz.

[11]: No. 306 Sqn ground crew under canvas at RAF Croydon.

[12]: No. 306 Squadron dispersal at RAF Croydon in June 1942.

[13–14]: No. 317 Sqn ground crew members pose with Spitfire VB BL860 JH-T 'Hala' (the Spitfire is discussed on pp. 28–29). Only LAC Zdzisław Dyrka, standing at the wing root, has been identified. Houses at Stafford Road in Croydon (nos. 230 to 244) can be seen in the background. They were still there at the time of writing.

[15]: To kill time while waiting for operation 'Rutter' to materialise, Polish ground crews at Croydon played volleyball…

[16]: …or cards. The tail of No. 317 Sqn Spitfire VB AD269 JH-B can be seen (compare photo [139] on p. 38). The nose of S/Ldr Tadeusz Nowierski's personal mount at the time, AB899 JH-G, can be seen in the background.

Polish Wings

[17–18]: Official signals of July 1942 with instructions to apply 'additional markings of experimental nature' in form of white stripes across the upper engine cowling panels and the top of the tailplane.

[19]: Another signal with orders to revert to standard markings.

[20–21]: Chalked markings on the nose of a No. 302 Sqn Spitfire VB (believed to be AA850) in preparation for the application of the white bands. The use of the English abbreviation of W for White (rather than Polish 'B for Biały') suggests that the painting on of these markings was done (or at least supervised) by the British staff at Croydon.

[22]: Replacing the engine on a No. 302 Sqn Spitfire VB (presumably BL990 WX-K, damaged during P/O Jerzy Paczuski's landing at Croydon on 3 July). Note the cowling panels with white stripes applied, positioned by the camouflaged wall behind the port wing.

17

AO/155 5/7 THE FOLLOWING SIGNAL RECEIVED FROM FIGHTER COMMAND BEGINS FOLLOWING ADDITIONAL MARKINGS ARE BEING ADOPTED FORTHWITH BY ALL DAY FIGHTER AIRCRAFT OPERATING IN NO 11 GROUP EXCEPTING MUSTANGS . THE NEW MARKINGS ARE OF EXPERIMENT NATURE AND MAY LATER BE ABANDONED . FOUR WHITE STRIPES NINE INCHES WIDE SEPARATED BY TWELVE INCHES NORMAL CAMOUFLAGE TO BE PAINTED ON ENGINE COWLINGS TERMINATING EACH END AT BOTTOM OF ENGINE SIDE PANELS . FIRST STRIPE TO BE TWELVE INCHES BEHIND SPINNER . TAILPLANE TO HAVE TWO STRIPES ONLY ON TOPSURFACES . FIRST STRIPE STARTING AT EXTREME TIPS . ALL OTHER CAMOUFLAGE AND MARKINGS NORMAL . MESSAGE ENDS

18

AO/160 7/7 .
FURTHER TO MY SIGNAL AO/155 5/7 AIRCRAFT AIRCRAFT SPINNER ALSO TO BE PAINTED WHITE . TAIL PLANES HAVE TWO STRIPES ON EACH SIDE OF RUDDER IN FORE AND AFT DIRECTION ON TOP SURFACES BMX ONLY ==1020

19

AO/184 14/7. REF MY AO/155 5/7 AND AO/160 7/7. SPECIAL ADDITIONAL MARKINGS ADOPTED FOR DAY FIGHTER AIRCRAFT OPERATING 11 GROUP HAVE BEEN ABANDONED. AIRCRAFT ARE REVERTING TO STANDARD MARKINGS FORTHWITH = 1832
POPE BBB

20

21

22

8

[23]: A flight of Polish Spitfires taking off from Croydon in July 1942. At least three of these aircraft, as well as the one parked in the foreground, display the white bands on the nose.

[24]: Engine test on a Supermarine- or Westland-built Spitfire VB of a Polish squadron, probably of No. 317, at Croydon in July 1942.

[25]: A CBAF-built Spitfire VB of No. 302 Sqn with the nose stripes washed off.

[26]: A well known photograph of AA853 WX-C with white bands on the nose. Such positioning of the codes, with the squadron letters WX between the roundel and the tail on both sides of the fuselage, was standard in No. 302 Sqn at the time. Despite incorrect captions in numerous publications this was not "the aircraft of W/Cdr Witorzeńc during Operation 'Jubilee' in August 1942"(all else aside, the officer did not participate in Operation 'Jubilee' in August, see the listings on pp. 87–90).

[27–28]: Two more shots of AA853 WX-C at Croydon in early July 1942. The tailplane white bands can just be made out on the leading edge. Note the prominent traces of replacing the early large under-wing roundel with a smaller late-style one. As opposed to all other day fighter units of the exiled Polish AF at the time, No. 302 Sqn applied the Polish national markings (white-red squares) near the cockpit.

[29]: Spitfire VB AA853 WX-C, No. 302 Squadron, Croydon, early July 1942. Upper surface camouflage: Ocean Grey and Dark Green ('A' pattern); under surface colour: Medium Sea Grey. Polish squares both sides of the fuselage near the cockpit. Special markings in form of white bands on the engine cowling and the horizontal tail surfaces.

[30]: *Spitfire VB AR336 UZ-O, No. 306 Squadron, Croydon, early July 1942. Upper surface camouflage: Ocean Grey and Dark Green ('A' pattern); under surface colour: Medium Sea Grey. Special markings in form of white bands on the engine cowling and the tailplane.*

[31]: *Spitfire VB AR336 UZ-O parked at Croydon in early July 1942 with the engine cowlings removed. The rearmost white nose band is prominent, and a single white band can be seen on the tailplane (but not on the elevator). No. 306 Sqn applied the codes on their Spitfires in the same layout as No. 302, with the unit letters UZ near the tail.*

11

Polish squadrons in Operation 'Jubilee'

As explained earlier, detailed description of Polish squadron operations on 19 August 1942 is beyond the scope of this book.

In a very brief summary of the day, the Polish Wing was well above the average. It provided 10% of the Spitfire squadrons engaged in the battle, suffered 3.5% of losses and was credited by Fighter Command with 17% of all enemy aircraft destroyed. Nos. 303 and 317 Polish Squadrons were the top-scoring units. Notably, they achieved this while still flying the Spitfire V variant, while some Fighter Command squadrons already had the much improved Mk IX.

The chapters that follow cover individual squadrons: first the two based at Northolt (Nos. 317 and 306), followed by those at Heston (Nos. 302 and 308), and ending with No. 303 at Redhill. Nos. 303 and 317 are given the broadest coverage, in view of their success in air combats that day.

Readers looking for an extensive account in English about the actions of Polish squadrons are encouraged to read the book by Norman Franks mentioned before. Polish speakers will want to read Grzegorz Śliżewski's 'Nad krwawiącymi liśćmi klonu. Polscy piloci myśliwscy w operacji „Jubilee"' ('Above the Bleeding Maple Leaves. Polish Fighter Pilots in Operation "Jubilee"').

An outline of operations of the Polish squadrons forms part of the documents reprinted in Appendix I. A listing of all operational sorties flown by Polish Spitfire squadrons that day is included in Appendix II. Personal combat reports' narratives are reprinted in Appendix III.

[32]: That week started on a high note at Northolt. The Polish AF Standard, made in secret in the occupied Poland and smuggled across the German-controlled Europe, rotated between Polish squadrons from July 1941 on, each hand-over being a major ceremony. On Monday 17 August 1942, No. 306 Sqn received it from No. 305 (Bomber) Squadron. Here, S/Ldr Tadeusz Czerwiński salutes the Standard now held by No. 306 Sqn colour party, led by P/O Józef Jeka (nearest camera). Each of these two pilots subsequently flew three sorties during 'Jubilee'. The squadron commander would die during a much less spectacular operation, just five days after this photograph was taken.

[33]: W/Cdr Tadeusz Rolski (left) visited Redhill on 17 August to discuss the forthcoming operation with S/Ldr Jan Zumbach (right). The readiness panel behind them shows '303' chalked on instead of the crossed out '611' (the RAF Squadron based there that moved to Kenley for the duration of 'Jubilee'). The list of 'B' Flight pilots can be deciphered: Marciniak (in Spitfire coded U) and Karczmarz (in T) in the 'Red' section, Adamek and Chojnacki in the 'Green' Section, Głowacki and Palak in the 'Black' one.

[34]: Press summary of the 1st Polish Wing's participation in 'Jubilee'. 'The famous Warsaw squadron' was No. 303; the pilot it lost was P/O Adam Damm; the one who landed 'with only one serviceable leg and one usable arm' was F/O Marian Cholewka of No. 317 Sqn. The Spitfire 'so full of cannon shells and bullet holes that it was almost a write-off' could be No. 303 Sqn's AR366 RF-C of Sgt Aleksander Rokitnicki or No. 317 Sqn's AA758 JH-V of Sgt Władysław Pawłowski.

THE POLES WADED IN: TOP SCORE AT DIEPPE

THE famous Warsaw squadron of the Polish Air Force, which destroyed 126 enemy aircraft in the Battle of Britain, was top scorer among the Allied fighter pilots who took part in the Battle of Dieppe.

Of the 91 German aircraft definitely destroyed in the operations, 38 fell to Allied pilots. Of these nine were shot down by the Warsaw squadron, and it also took part in the destruction of a tenth.

These victories were scored for the loss of only one of the squadron's pilots.

One Polish pilot was wounded in the right arm and leg, but with only one serviceable leg and one usable arm he made a perfect landing on the south coast.

Lucky escape

He lost consciousness twice during the journey home, and was again unconscious when the mechanics reached him after he landed.

One of his countrymen, who became separated from his companions, was attacked time after time by F.W.190s. They filled his Spitfire so full of cannon-shell and bullet holes that it was almost a write-off when he landed.

Yet he climbed out of his aircraft without so much as having suffered a cut finger.

[35]: P/O Mirosław Maciejowski from No. 317 Sqn was the Polish top-scorer of 'Jubilee' with two and one shared enemy aircraft destroyed to his credit. On the debit side, at the end of his last sortie he belly landed Spitfire VB BL927 JH-L at Northolt "forgetting to use emergency appliances when his plane's undercarriage would not open" (as the accident report put it). It took a month to make the Spitfire airworthy again. Such accidents were not unusual among seasoned pilots whose human endurance was at its limits. Maciejowski had served continuously with operational squadrons since September 1940 (!) as an NCO pilot, earning a commission in June 1942. A week after 'Jubilee' he was finally posted for a period of rest as an instructor at an Operational Training Unit.

[36]: Following his last sortie with No. 317 Sqn before the posting, Maciejowski was given a fitting farewell toast: note how the glasses are arranged in various squadron formations! F/O Teofil Szymankiewicz is seated on the left, F/O Zbigniew Janicki stands behind him, P/O Stanisław Brzeski is at the end of the table and F/O Lech Xiężopolski is pouring wine.

[37]: F/Lt Wieńczysław Barański was one of No. 308 Squadron ground controllers at the Northolt Sector Operations Room, but he flew a sortie with No. 306 Sqn during 'Jubilee' (it was simpler to join a Northolt-based unit than travel to his squadron's base at Heston). Soon after 'Jubilee' he was posted as a flight commander to No. 302 Sqn.

Apart from those of the 1st Wing, five Polish pilots flew with non-Polish squadrons during 'Jubilee'. Two were with No. 403 Squadron RCAF on Spitfire Vs and three with the Hurricane II-equipped No. 87 Squadron RAF:

[38]: F/O Andrzej Malarowski flew two sorties with No. 87 Sqn. Oddly, his second one was mistakenly omitted in the unit Operations Record Book (ORB), which mentions 12 pilots participating, but only quotes 11 names.

[39]: P/O Jan Mozołowski flew two sorties with No. 403 Sqn.

[40]: F/O Antoni Waltoś was shot down during his first sortie with No. 87 Sqn. His body was never found. He was the first of two Polish pilots killed during 'Jubilee'.

[41]: F/O Jan Wiejski flew one sortie with No. 403 Sqn.

[42]: F/O Edward Witke flew one sortie with No. 87 Sqn.

No. 317 Squadron (RAF Northolt)

At the time of 'Jubilee' No. 317 was the 'senior' squadron at Northolt, having been based there since April 1942. As it used the dispersal located nearest the Officers' Mess, its ground staff was responsible for the maintenance of the Spitfires used by the Wing Leader and his deputy. When senior officers joined the Wing on operations, as it happened repeatedly during 'Jubilee', they used No. 317 Sqn aircraft.

At the time of 'Jubilee' the squadron was commanded by S/Ldr Stanisław Skalski, eventually the top-scoring Polish ace of WW2. Notably, focused on leading his men rather than on his personal achievements, he claimed no victories as a squadron commander (either with No. 317 or later with No. 601 RAF in the Mediterranean). His flight commanders were F/Lt Marian Trzebiński and F/Lt Kazimierz Rutkowski. F/Lts Jan Wiśniewski and Tadeusz Kumiega were No. 317 Sqn Operations Room controllers, an important (but usually forgotten) duty for a fighter unit in those days.

No. 317 flew four missions during 'Jubilee', starting in the early morning. The squadron suffered the first Polish casualty that day, when F/O Marian Cholewka was badly injured in a surprise attack by Focke-Wulfs about 6 a.m. He managed to reach Britain and land his Spitfire AR340 JH-P safely.

[43–48]: Photos taken at Northolt following the afternoon mission, when six pilots claimed three individual and three shared 'kills'.

[43]: Upon his arrival from the operation W/Cdr Stefan Janus talks to pilots who had not participated in this patrol. Left to right in the foreground: F/O Przesław Sadowski, F/O Teofil Szymankiewicz (behind him), W/Cdr Janus, G/Cpt Alfred Guy Adnams, unrecognised ground crew member, F/Sgt Tadeusz Hanzelka, and F/O Jerzy Mencel. Although G/Cpt Adnams is wearing Mae-West, no known document mentions him flying on operations that day.

[44]: S/Ldr Skalski (far right) joins the group and talks to W/Cdr Janus and G/Cpt Adnams.

[45]: S/Ldr Skalski talking to the senior officers. Ground crew members are listening carefully, including LAC Ludwik Krzyżosiak (partly obscured by Skalski's profile).

[46-47]: F/O Mencel moves back while P/O Stanisław Łukaszewicz (wearing Mae-West) joins the conversation.

[48]: Skalski now talks to Łukaszewicz, with Krzyżosiak between the two pilots.

During the second and fourth missions, No. 317 Sqn pilots scored seven and one shared German aircraft destroyed, the second best result of Fighter Command that day. One Spitfire, AA758 JH-V, was badly shot up in these combats. Another aircraft, BL927 JH-L, was seriously damaged in a landing accident of P/O Mirosław Maciejowski upon return from the unit's last mission that day.

[49]: *More pilots who had just landed. Left to right in the foreground: P/O Łukaszewicz, F/Lt Kazimierz Rutkowski ('B' Flight Commander), Sgt Wacław Frączek and F/Sgt Kazimierz Sztramko.*

[50]: *F/Lt Marian Trzebiński, No. 317 Sqn 'A' Flight Commander, is 'smiled' by F/Lt Rutkowski (right) and P/O Łukaszewicz. None of the squadron's victories on 19 August were scored when Trzebiński was flying. Moreover, P/O Łukaszewicz flew Trzebiński's personal Spitfire AR424 JH-A 'Ewunia' when he claimed a Focke-Wulf 190 destroyed during the mission immediately preceding this photo!*

[51]: *Still in their Mae-Wests, P/O Stanisław Brzeski (in the middle) and W/Cdr Tadeusz Rolski (right).*

[52]: *F/Lt Kazimierz Rutkowski in No. 317 Sqn dispersal, with the Officers' Mess behind him. Two Spitfires can be seen: BL860 JH-T on the left and BM566 JH-S on the right. W/ Cdr Rolski had just landed in BL860 and P/O Brzeski had just used BM566 to claim a He 111 destroyed. Note that BM566 is not mentioned in No. 317 Sqn ORB, which has a number of entries for 'S 332'. AR332 had, indeed, been coded JH-S, but failed to return on 29 April 1942! No. 317 Sqn ORB is notorious for such errors throughout 1942, using 'ghost' serials of Spitfires long lost rather than current ones that bore the same code.*

[53–59]: More photos taken at the same occasion, after No. 317 Sqn Intelligence Officer joined the group to note down the reports of individual pilots.

[53]: Skalski lights a cigarette, while P/O Stanisław Brzeski can be seen on the right, describing his victory.

[54]: F/O Edmund Sienkiewicz, the IO, takes notes as P/O Michał Maciejowski (wearing his Mae-West) tells about his combat.

[55]: Sgt Adam Kolczyński talks and gesticulates to the IO. Listening carefully behind him are LAC Józef Waśniowski (far left) and Cpl Władysław Brzózkiewicz (in peaked cap).

[56]: P/O Łukaszewicz gives his report in a particularly entertaining way.

[57]: Five victorious pilots compare their notes, left to right in the foreground: P/O Brzeski, Sgt Kolczyński, P/O Maciejowski, P/O Łukaszewicz and F/Lt Rutkowski.

[58]: Sgt Wacław Frączek (far left) listening to the discussion between P/O Brzeski and Sgt Kolczyński, while P/O Maciejowski enjoys his cigarette.

[59]: P/O Brzeski and Sgt Kolczyński continue their discussion. Meanwhile, F/O Roman Hrycak has joined the group and is standing between P/Os Maciejowski and Łukaszewicz.

[60]: *Spitfire BL410 JH-D, flown by F/O Hrycak during that mission, as backdrop for F/Sgt Julian Faliński, 'A' Flight's Chief Mechanic (third left), Sgt Kazimierz Owsianka (standing third right) and their men. This photo was taken a few months before 'Jubilee', while the under-wing roundels were still in the old style.*

[61]: *S/Ldr Wojciech Kołaczkowski, who had commanded No. 303 Sqn until May 1942, was another Polish Ops Officer at HQ No. 11 Group at Uxbridge that summer. Just like W/Cdr Rolski, he also used to join the 1st Wing on operations. Here he leaves No. 317 Sqn Spitfire BL860 JH-T 'Hala' in July or August.*

[62–63]: *S/Ldr Kołaczkowski flew one sortie over Dieppe during 'Jubilee', using No. 317 Sqn Spitfire EN896 JH-X. These photos were taken at Northolt on 14 June 1942 during a publicity event promoting Polish-US alliance. Note that the fuselage roundel is in the later style (known informally as 'C1'), while the underwing one still has the old dimensions and proportions ('A'). The former markings (and the fin flashes) had been modified by mid-June on the Spitfires of the 1st Wing but the latter insignia were not changed until late June/early July. The nominal Ocean Grey on EN896 looks rather too pale, while that on the nose of the other Spitfire is definitely too dark.*

[64]: *No. 317 Sqn Spitfires taking off from Northolt in the summer of 1942. Squadron-strength take-offs were not unusual in those days, using the whole width of the grass aerodrome, not just the concrete runway. In the group nearest camera three Spitfires can be made out: JH-Q (BM131), JH-Z (BL690) and JH-V (AA758), all described in detail in this book. Note the hangar, with the peculiar colour scheme supposed to imitate rows of houses and gardens typical for London suburbs.*

[65-67]: EN916 was the personal mount of W/Cdr Stefan Janus. During late June 1942 W/Cdr Janus flew to RAF Woodvale to visit No. 315 Sqn, a unit he had commanded before becoming the Wing Leader at Northolt. Before his flight back his Spitfire was covered with chalked messages from No. 315 Sqn to their Northolt friends. These photos were taken before departure from Woodvale. The group of No. 315 Squadron personnel inspecting the 'air mail' in [66] includes three pilots at far left. Left to right: P/O Lech Kondracki, Sgt Marek Słoński and F/O Czesław Tarkowski.

[68]: This photo was taken upon arrival at Northolt, while the 'air mail' was studied. F/Sgt Jan Malinowski from No. 317 Sqn is standing near the wing leading edge (with a white scarf around his neck), with Sgt Piotr Kuryłłowicz immediately behind him.

[69] The port side of the Spitfire. F/Sgt Jan Malinowski and Sgt Piotr Kuryłłowicz are now standing between the fuselage and the starboard wing. The position of the Polish AF marking below the first section of exhausts was standard for No. 303 Sqn, who had serviced the Spitfire until mid-June 1942.

[70] Starboard side of EN916, with Sgt Piotr Kuryłłowicz standing in front. Sadly, the meaning of individual messages is virtually lost now, as the pun in them was only comprehensible for the senders and the recipients.

[71]: An unrecognised member of No. 317 Sqn ground staff on the open cockpit of EN916. It had started its career in the care of No. 303 Sqn, and was coded RF-J initially. After that unit departed Northolt in mid-June 1942, it was taken over by the ground crew of No. 317, becoming JH-J. The new unit code was applied over crudely overpainted RF, as shown by the patch of a darker shade beneath the H and a part of J.

[72]: After a while, No. 317 Sqn badge was added below the windscreen on both sides of the Spitfire (the standard position of this emblem from the spring 1942 on). Standing by the aeroplane, left to right: possibly AC1 Wincenty Manicki, F/O Konstanty Świerczyński (squadron ground defence officer), F/Sgt Jan Malinowski and possibly Cpl Michał Bodnar.

[73]: EN916 photographed in late June or early July 1942, possibly at Croydon, during replacing of the old-style under-wing roundels with the new ones. Notably, the fuselage roundels and fin flashes had been changed a couple weeks before that.

[74]: Spitfire VB EN916 JH-J, of W/Cdr Stefan Janus, Northolt Wing Leader, 3 sorties during 'Jubilee'. Upper surface camouflage: Ocean Grey and Dark Green ('A' pattern); under surface colour: Medium Sea Grey. Polish squares both sides of the nose. No. 317 Sqn badge below the windscreen.

77

75

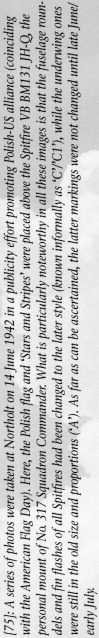

76

[75]: A series of photos were taken at Northolt on 14 June 1942 in a publicity effort promoting Polish-US alliance (coinciding with the American Flag Day). Here, the Polish flag and 'Stars and Stripes' were placed above the Spitfire VB BM131 JH-Q, the personal mount of No 317 Squadron Commander. What is particularly noteworthy in all these images is that the fuselage roundels and fin flashes of all Spitfires had been changed to the later style (known informally as 'C'/'C1'), while the underwing ones were still in the old size and proportions ('A'). As far as can be ascertained, the latter markings were not changed until late June/early July.

[76]: An informal shot of four members of No. 317 Sqn ground crew with BM131 JH-Q and the flags. Standing at the top is Cpl Stefan Kalisz-Kalisiak, the squadron photographer. Holding the blade are Cpl Jan Hołdak, armourer (right) and possibly Sgt Paulin Pszczółkowski, RAF Northolt Station photographer.

[77]: BM131 JH-Q in less shiny condition, parked behind a soldier of the aerodrome AA defence and his gun.

78

[78]: Spitfire VB BM131 JH-Q, No. 317 Squadron, Northolt. 4 sorties during 'Jubilee'. Upper surface camouflage: Ocean Grey and Dark Green ('A' pattern); under surface colour: Medium Sea Grey. Polish squares both sides of the nose, with 'POLAND' stencil underneath. No. 317 Sqn badge below the windscreen on both sides of the fuselage.

[79]: S/Ldr Skalski taxies his mount out of his allocated parking spot. Note BL860 JH-T further on the left.

[80]: Skalski leaves the cockpit upon landing, while a ground crew member is already refuelling it. According to captions in squadron diaries, both these photos were taken on 19 August 1942.

[81]: F/O Stanisław Bochniak flew BM131 JH-Q during the first afternoon mission, as his usual mount, BL860 JH-T 'Hala', was used by W/Cdr Rolski on that occasion.

[82–83]: BM131 parked in front of No. 317 Sqn dispersal hut at RAF Northolt, not far from the Officers' Mess. Skalski personally test flew the newly delivered Spitfire on 7 May 1942, a day after he took command of No. 317. The code JH-Q was not chosen at random. Aircraft letters were usually linked with girls' names in Polish squadrons, but Q is not used in Polish, so there was no matching name. Due to the Polish pronunciation of the letter as 'koo' it was commonly linked with the word 'kukułka' (cuckoo). Since Skalski had not flown with No. 317 Sqn before taking command of it (unlike his predecessors at this post), he was seen as a 'cuckoo's egg', which led to this code being adopted for his personal Spitfire.

[84]: *Spitfire VB AR424 JH-A, No. 317 Squadron, Northolt. 4 sorties and 1-0-0 victories during 'Jubilee'. Upper surface camouflage: Ocean Grey and Dark Green ('A' pattern); under surface colour: Medium Sea Grey. Polish squares both sides of the nose, with 'POLAND' stencil underneath. 'Ewunia' personal name applied on both sides of the fuselage forward of the cockpit.*

[85]: *The engine of AR424 JH-A is test-run at No. 317 Sqn dispersal at Northolt. At the time it was usual for the 'A' and 'B' Flight Commanders' aircraft to be coded JH-A and JH-Z, respectively.*

[86]: *F/O Teofil Szymankiewicz on the nose of the Spitfire. The stencil-style aircraft letter on the lower cowling is shown to advantage.*

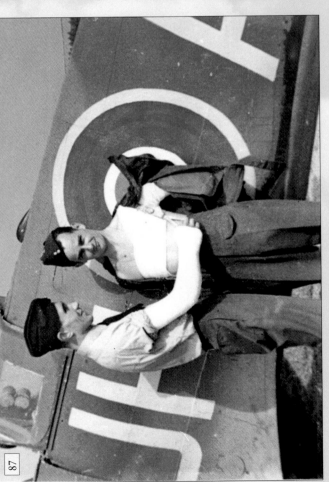

[87]: F/O Władysław Pucek (left) had a serious crash in BL802 JH-J on 17 May 1942 while returning from a sweep over France, while F/Lt Marian Trzebiński (right) pranged his first JH-A, AD397, on 1 June. This photograph was taken during June, while both were recovering from their injuries. Note the 'C1' fuselage roundel on AR424, with recently overpainted portions of yellow and white rings of the earlier 'A1' style.

[88]: Another shot of F/O Pucek, with his right arm in plaster, and F/Lt Trzebiński in front of AR424.

[89]: Close up of the nose, with the Polish national marking and the personal name 'Ewunia' ('Little Eva'), applied in honour of Trzebiński's wife.

[90]: *Spitfire VB BL690 JH-Z, No. 317 Squadron, Northolt. 2 sorties and 1-0-0 victories during 'Jubilee'. Upper surface camouflage: Ocean Grey and Dark Green ('A' pattern); under surface colour: Medium Sea Grey. Polish squares both sides of the nose, with 'POLAND' stencil underneath. No. 317 Sqn badge below the wind-screen (possibly port side only).*

[91]: BL690 JH-Z refuelled in No. 317 Sqn dispersal from a standard bowser trailer. The squadron badge below the windscreen can be seen. The under-wing roundel is in 'C' size and style, with noticeable traces of a large 'A' one overpainted beneath.

[92]: BL690 JH-Z was the personal mount of F/Lt Kazimierz Rutkowski, shown here talking to LAC Wiktor Piwowarczyk by the side of the Spitfire.

[93–95]: Three photos of F/O Marian Cholewka with BL690 JH-Z at Northolt in June 1942. These are orthochromatic images, rendering the standard roundel tones in an unusual way, and also exaggerating the exhaust residue effect on the side of the fuselage. EN919 JH-N, seen in the background, was seriously damaged on 7 July 1942, when landing at Northolt back from Croydon (Sgt Piotr Kuryłłowicz escaped unhurt), and did not return to No. 317 Sqn before their departure from Northolt in September.

[96]: *Spitfire VB BL860 JH-T at Northolt in the spring of 1942, before the British national markings were modified. The four ground crew members in front of the aeroplane are, left to right: Cpls Franciszek Kujawiński, Adam Kozów, Władysław Brzózkiewicz and unrecognised. The dark appearance of the outer ring of the roundel shows that this is an orthochromatic photo. A part of the Spitfire's individual name can be made out to the right of Brzózkiewicz's head, presumably in pale yellow.*

[97]: *Spitfire VB BL860 JH-T, No. 317 Squadron, Northolt. 4 sorties and 0-0-2 victories during 'Jubilee'. Upper surface camouflage: Ocean Grey and Dark Green ('A' pattern); under surface colour: Medium Sea Grey. Polish squares both sides of the nose, with 'POLAND' stencil underneath. 'Hala' ('Little Halina') personal name applied on both sides of the fuselage forward of the cockpit. No. 317 Sqn badge below the windscreen, starboard side only.*

[98]: *BL860 photographed during the summer of 1942, after the change in RAF markings. Sadly, only two individuals have been identified in the group: standing first right on the ground is LAC Józef Waśniowski, while second right is S/Ldr Walenty Nowacki, the Roman Catholic padre at RAF Northolt.*

28

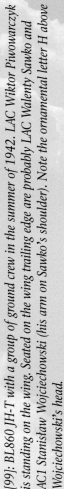

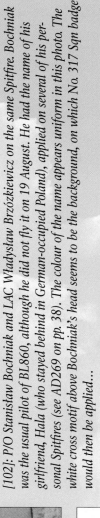

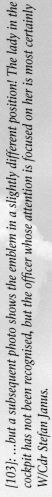

[99]: BL860 JH-T with a group of ground crew in the summer of 1942. LAC Wiktor Piwowarczyk is standing on the wing. Seated on the wing trailing edge are probably LAC Walenty Sawko and AC1 Stanisław Wojciechowski (his arm on Sawko's shoulder). Note the ornamental letter H above Wojciechowski's head.

[100]: The close-up of LAC Jan Smółka taken on the same occasion shows that the very pale letter H (presumably white) was followed by the rest of the name 'Hala' in darker characters (presumably yellow). It is not clear whether this two-tone style was a permanent one, or if these photos were taken while the inscription was being repainted from one colour to the other.

[101]: F/O Florian Martini flew the Spitfire's first sortie during 'Jubilee', between 5 and 7 a.m.

[102]: P/O Stanisław Bochniak and LAC Władysław Brzózkiewicz on the same Spitfire. Bochniak was the usual pilot of BL860, although he did not fly it on 19 August. He had the name of his girlfriend, Hala (who stayed behind in German-occupied Poland), applied on several of his personal Spitfires (see AD269 on pp. 38). The colour of the name appears uniform in this photo. The white cross motif above Bochniak's head seems to be the background, on which No. 317 Sqn badge would then be applied...

[103]: ...but a subsequent photo shows the emblem in a slightly different position! The lady in the cockpit has not been recognised, but the officer whose attention is focused on her is most certainly W/Cdr Stefan Janus.

[104]: Another photo taken on the same occasion shows the name 'Hala' on the port side, but not the squadron badge.

[105]: Spitfire VB AR340 JH-P, No. 317 Squadron, Northolt. 1 sortie during 'Jubilee', seriously damaged in combat. Upper surface camouflage: Ocean Grey and Dark Green ('A' pattern); under surface colour: Medium Sea Grey. Polish squares both sides of the nose, with 'POLAND' stencil underneath. No. 317 Sqn badge below the windscreen on both sides of the fuselage.

[106]: F/Sgt Tadeusz Hanzelka 'riding' AR340 at Northolt in the summer of 1942. The serial number seems partly obliterated, possibly during some minor repairs to rear fuselage.

[107]: Sgt Jan Malinowski on the wing of the same Spitfire. On 20 July 1942 he flew AR340 during a 'Rhubarb' over France when it was damaged by Flak.

[108]: A slightly blurred photo showing AR340 JH-P with the altered-style serial. Standing in the middle of the group is Sgt Jan Malinowski, who flew the Spitfire's last operational sortie with No. 317 Sqn on 29 August, following repairs after 'Jubilee'.

[109]: A member of the ground crew, possibly AC2 Mieczysław Kolka, posing with AR340. The serial number has been reapplied during some more repair, probably in the wake of the dramatic sortie of F/O Cholewka on 19 August.

[110]: Left to right: S/Ldr Skalski, G/Cpt Adnams, W/Cdr Rolski and F/Lt Rutkowski in discussion at Northolt, with AR340 JH-P in the distance.

[111]: F/O Marian Cholewka (far right) flew AR340's only sortie during 'Jubilee'. At about 6 a.m. a direct hit in the cockpit heavily wounded his right arm, his right leg was also hit. He managed to reach Britain and landed at Lympne, but had to be lifted out of the cockpit. His convalescence took a long time, he was eventually able to resume operational flying in June 1945. This photo was taken in December 1942 when he visited Northolt. Second right is Francis Gabreski, at the time an inexperienced USAAF pilot of Polish descent who volunteered to fly with Polish squadrons to learn the basics of fighter flying. He ended the war as the top-scoring American ace of the European theatre. The other officers in the photo are W/Cdr Stefan Janus (second left) and P/O Tadeusz Seemann, RAF Northolt Motor Transport Officer. The Spitfire VB behind them is ZF-Z from No. 308 Sqn (probably EP171, flown by F/Lt Jerzy Popławski during 'Jubilee').

[112]: Pilot Sgt Michał Maciejowski (left) and LAC Jan Ziemierowski standing in front of Spitfire VB AA758 JH-V (with unrecognised 'erk' on the cockpit door). When this photo was taken in early spring 1942, AA758 was the personal mount of S/Ldr Piotr Ozyra, commanding No. 317 Sqn, and his nickname, 'Bazyli Kwiek', was applied on both sides below the windscreen (similar to 'Hesio' on his predecessor's Spitfires – see PW 30). The unit badge was applied aft of the cockpit canopy, its standard position on Spitfires delivered to No. 317 in 1941. Note the finish peeling off near the cockpit door.

[113]: Spitfire VB AA758 JH-V, No. 317 Squadron, Northolt. 1 sortie during 'Jubilee', seriously damaged in combat. Upper surface camouflage: unspecified dark grey and Dark Green ('A' pattern); under surface colour: Medium Sea Grey. Polish squares both sides of the nose, with 'POLAND' stencil underneath. No. 317 Sqn badge aft of the cockpit on both sides of the fuselage. 'Bazyli Kwiek' (nickname of S/Ldr Piotr Ozyra) personal name applied on the port side of the fuselage forward of the cockpit.

[114–115]: F/O Witold Łanowski with AA758 in the summer of 1942. During June the Spitfire was repainted, and Ocean Grey was replaced by a distinctively darker hue. The 'Bazyli Kwiek' inscription was reapplied in larger size and further forward, probably on the port side only. In photo [115]: Łanowski is accompanied by ground crew members, of whom only Cpl Edward Ancuta (first right) could be identified.

[116]: F/Lt Rutkowski, W/Cdr Janus and S/Ldr Nowierski inspect the Flak damage to AA758 after a Rhubarb over France on 24 July 1942. The tail surfaces were badly shot up, but F/O Łanowski managed to get back to Northolt. Note the absence of the 'Bazyli Kwiek' inscription on the starboard side of the fuselage.

[117]: Unrecognised ground crew with the shot up Spitfire. Note the position of the serial number and code letter on this side.

[118]: Sgt Władysław Pawłowski flew AA758's sole sortie during 'Jubilee'. He claimed a Focke-Wulf damaged at about 10.30 a.m., but his Spitfire was badly shot up in the process and he barely made it back to base. It had to be sent away for repairs and that terminated its connection with the Polish Air Force.

[119]: The port side of the tail photographed at Croydon in early July 1942.

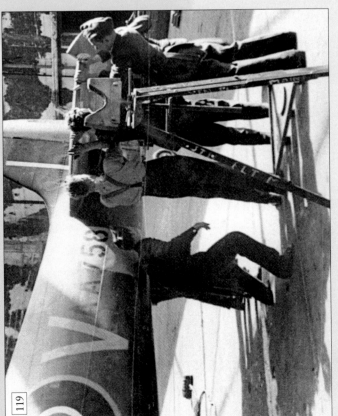

[120–121]: F/O Teofil Szymankiewicz (in flying gear) and two unrecognised ground crew members with AB925 JH-F in early 1942. Note the blister fairing on the starboard side of the nose, standard on early CBAF production Mk Vs. The aircraft is in standard Day Fighter Scheme camouflage with soft division lines between Dark Green and Ocean Grey. BL927 JH-L can be seen in photo [121]; and the camouflage tones of both aircraft look pretty similar.

[122–123]: AB925 JH-F in the summer 1942, with visiting sailors of the exiled Polish Navy. The group in [123]: includes LAC Wincenty Szatkowski (third left) and Cpl Stanisław Baran (seventh left). By the time of these photos the Ocean Grey areas had been repainted with a distinctively paler grey, presumably using hand brush that gave an uneven coat of paint and rather sharp colour division lines. Note the newly fitted Malcolm hood with unpainted framing.

121

123

120

122

[124] Spitfire VB AB925 JH-F, No. 317 Squadron, Northolt. 4 sorties during 'Jubilee'.
Upper surface camouflage: unspecified pale grey and Dark Green ('A' pattern); under surface colour: Medium Sea Grey. Polish squares both sides of the nose, with 'POLAND' stencil underneath.

124

[125]: Spitfire VB AD295 JH-C, No. 317 Squadron, Northolt. 3 sorties and ⅓-0-0 victories during 'Jubilee'. Upper surface camouflage: unspecified dark grey and Dark Green ('A' pattern); under surface colour: Medium Sea Grey. Polish squares both sides of the nose, with 'POLAND' stencil underneath. No. 317 Sqn badge aft of the cockpit on both sides of the fuselage.

[126]: No. 317 Sqn Spitfires about to take off from Northolt in the summer of 1942. The group includes AD295 JH-C at far left and AB925 JH-F second right. It is noteworthy how the camouflage tones on JH-C seem darker and those on JH-F paler than on the other two.

[127]: No. 317 Squadron temporary dispersal at Croydon in the first days of July 1942. The group in the foreground includes Cpl Jan Hołdak at far left and Feluś the dog on the right (the others have, sadly, not been identified). Spitfire VBs AB925 JH-F, AD295 JH-C and BL927 JH-L are lined up along the taxiway. All three have Malcolm hoods, sunlight reflecting from their bulged transparencies. The hood framing on AB925 is unpainted. Note how the grey of the camouflage on JH-F looks pale and that on JH-C dark compared to the standard tones on JH-L. The nose on the right is probably that of AD269 JH-B. Backdrop is provided by houses at Stafford Road (nos. 212 to 242).

125

126

127

[128]: Cpl Franciszek Szafrański (left) and another ground crew member by the nose of AB925 JH-F in early 1942 (on the same occasion as [121]:), with BL927 JH-L in the background.

[129]: A group of ground crew with BL927 at the same time. Cpl Jan Hołdak is far left and LAC Jan Ziemierowski at far right on the wing.

[130]: BL927 taxiing at Northolt. At the time the Spitfire still displayed the early British markings ('A'/'A1') and no squadron badge.

[131]: Another souvenir shot. AC1 Antoni Rydzewski is on the nose, AC1 Jan Awdziejew in the cockpit, LAC Władysław Wodczyński standing first right, and AC1 Stanisław Byszyński next to him. In this orthochromatic image the blue ring of the roundel is rendered unnaturally pale.

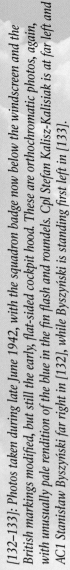

[132–133]: Photos taken during late June 1942, with the squadron badge now below the windscreen and the British markings modified, but still the early, flat-sided cockpit hood. These are orthochromatic photos, again, with unusually pale rendition of the blue in the fin flash and roundels. Cpl Stefan Kalisz-Kalisiak is at far left and AC1 Stanisław Byszyński far right in [132], while Byszyński is standing first left in [133].

[134]: Ground crew (Cpl Jan Hołdak in the middle) with BL927 at Croydon in early July 1942.

[135]: Spitfire VB BL927 JH-L, No. 317 Squadron, Northolt. 4 sorties and 2½-0-0 victories during 'Jubilee', seriously damaged in a landing accident. Upper surface camouflage: Ocean Grey and Dark Green ('A' pattern); under surface colour: Medium Sea Grey. Polish squares both sides of the nose, with 'POLAND' stencil underneath. No. 317 Sqn badge below the windscreen on both sides of the fuselage.

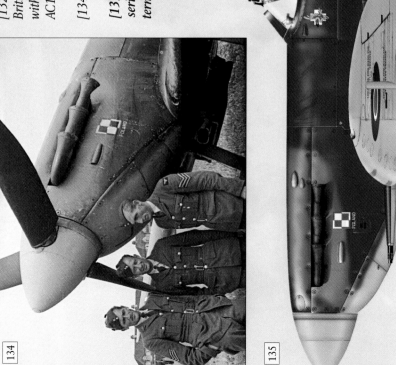

[136]: Cpl Bronisław Szatajko in the cockpit of AD269 JH-B. The squadron badge was in a style and position typical for Spitfires delivered to No. 317 Sqn in 1941. This was the usual mount of P/O Stanisław Bochniak until the end of March 1942 and displayed the name 'Hala' (that of his girlfriend) forward of the cockpit. In April the pilot was re-posted to 'B' Flight and had the name transferred onto BL860 JH-T (see pp. 28–29).

[137–138]: Spitfire VB AD269 JH-B at Northolt in the early spring of 1942. The spot where 'Hala' was obliterated below the windscreen can be made out in photo [137]. LAC Stanisław Krysztofiak is first right in both photos.

[139]: A group of ground crew play cards by the tail of AD269 at Croydon in early July 1942 (compare photo [16]: on p.7). LAC Stanisław Baliga is looking at his cards, seated directly below the digits 69 of the serial number. Cpl Edward Ancuta is sitting to the right of him. AC1 Jan Kurc is kneeling in front of the rudder looking at the photographer. The sharp colour division line and absence of any stencilling on the rudder suggest it was repaired or replaced and repainted. R7296 JH-I can be seen in the background. It was a very old aeroplane by wartime standards, having been built in March 1941 as one of the first Mk Vs. It failed to participate in 'Jubilee', damaged in an accident in July and sent away for repairs.

[140]: AC1 Stanisław Byszyński by the starboard side of AD269 JH-B.

[141]: Close-up of the old-style badge of No. 317 Sqn, as applied on Spitfires delivered in late 1941. Recent research shows that its colours were quite different from those used in the later variant of the emblem, but the actual hues of the early one are not known.

[142]: Spitfire VB AD269 JH-B, No. 317 Squadron, Northolt. 4 sorties and ½-0-0 victories during 'Jubilee'. Upper surface camouflage: Ocean Grey and Dark Green ('A' pattern); under surface colour: Medium Sea Grey. Polish squares both sides of the nose, with 'POLAND' stencil underneath. No. 317 Sqn badge aft of the cockpit on both sides of the fuselage.

No. 306 Squadron (RAF Northolt)

No. 306 was the other squadron at Northolt, based there since mid-June 1942. It was commanded by S/Ldr Tadeusz Czerwiński, with F/Lts Józef Gil and Józef Żulikowski as flight commanders, and F/Lts Jan Pentz and Karol Pniak as Ops Room controllers.

The squadron, sadly, fared worst of the entire 1st Polish Wing during 'Jubilee'. It suffered the first Polish Spitfire write-off of the operation, when Sgt Stefan Czachla force-landed in a street not far from RAF Northolt about 7 a.m. Fortunately the pilot was not badly injured. F/O Bohdan Arct's Spitfire VB AR337 UZ-A was damaged by Flak about midday, during the unit's second mission, but the pilot landed safely at Northolt. The third mission was cancelled shortly after take-off. Finally, during its fourth mission, No. 306 lost F/O Emil Landsman, when his BM424 UZ-S was shot down into the Channel about 5 p.m. The pilot was rescued by the Germans and spent the rest of the war as a PoW. Additionally, No. 306 Sqn flew an uneventful two-aircraft scramble over Northolt in the afternoon.

[143]: S/Ldr Tadeusz Czerwiński, commanding No. 306 Squadron, flew three sorties during 'Jubilee'.

[144]: 'A' Flight Commander F/Lt Józef Gil flew two operational sorties on 19 August 1942.

[145]: 'B' Flight Commander F/Lt Józef Żulikowski flew one sortie during 'Jubilee'.

[146]: Nine NCO pilots of No. 306 Sqn in the summer of 1942. Standing, left to right: F/Sgt Marcin Machowiak, Sgt Stefan Czachla, Sgt Marian Kordasiewicz, F/Sgt Witold Krupa and F/Sgt Brunon Kroczyński; seated on the stairs, left to right: F/Sgt Wawrzyniec Jasiński, Sgt Jan Paweł Gajewski, F/Sgt Zdzisław Horn and Sgt Jan Aleksander Rogowski (not to be confused with the Battle of Britain participant also named Jan Rogowski).

[147]: A group of officer pilots of No. 306 Sqn in the summer of 1942, left to right: F/Lt Żulikowski, F/O Emil Landsman, F/O Bohdan Arct, P/O Jerzy Polak, P/O Władysław Potocki, F/O Stanisław Marcisz, F/O Antoni Krąkowski.

[148]: *The first Spitfire lost by the 1ˢᵗ Polish Wing during 'Jubilee': AD581 UZ-M written off about 7.15 in Malvern Avenue, South Harrow, some 2,000 m from the Northolt aerodrome, when Sgt Stefan Czachla [149] attempted a forced landing due to lack of fuel. A contemporary press reporter described the circumstances: 'After hitting the top of No. 205, it lost a wheel, cannoned to the opposite side of the road, and one of its wings then ripped along the front bedrooms of Nos. 244, 246, 248, 250 and 252, the plane finishing in the front garden of No. 252. Nobody was seriously hurt and the pilot received only minor cuts.' A young lady who lived at No. 250 wrote that afternoon: 'I was lying in bed when I heard a plane flying low, but as that is a normal occurrence I took no notice. The next second all I knew was that glass, bricks & pieces of furniture & a cloud of dust was coming on top of me.[…] It was a fighter plane which had run out of petrol & had to make a forced landing. Five houses are damaged, Mr Wells being the worst. The pilot had a cut head & Anne was badly bruised on the elbow & ribs & is in hospital, but other than that there were no injuries, which is remarkable considering the damage done. Our house looks very sorry for itself in the front, although the back is completely undamaged. […] The Rescue squads, Fire Brigade & RAF arrived almost at once & by now, 4.30p.m., most of the plane has been removed & they are now covering our front with tarpaulin. The electricity is cut off, so shall have to go to bed early tonight.' Another neighbour, woken up when the Spitfire wingtip shattered his bedroom window, apparently just remarked to his wife 'You can't get any bloody privacy these days'. Years later, this crash landing had profound consequences for John Dibbs, who would become a renowned aviation photographer. To quote him from the book 'Spitfire. The Official Companion to the Feature Documentary': 'My late father, John Snr, was a young boy at the time and lived a couple of streets away. He and many others rushed to the crash site to find the Spitfire in the front garden of a house, with its port wing tip resting against the upstairs bay window. […] Thirty odd years later, my father took me to the site and regaled me with the story. This ignited in me an enduring passion and fascination for World War Two aviation and in particular the 'Spit'.'*

[150]: *F/O Emil Landsman flew three sorties during 'Jubilee'. About 16.30, he was shot down in air combat over the returning convoy. He managed to use his dinghy, and was picked up by a German torpedo boat around midnight. He spent the rest of the war in captivity. This photo was taken in 1943 at the Stalag Luft 3 at Sagan (now Żagań, Poland).*

[151]: *Spitfire VB AA930 UZ-P, No. 306 Squadron, Northolt. 2 sorties during 'Jubilee'. Upper surface camouflage: Ocean Grey and Dark Green ('A' pattern); under surface colour: Medium Sea Grey. Polish squares both sides of the nose, with 'POLAND' stencil underneath. No. 306 Sqn badge below the windscreen.*

151

153

152

[152–154]: A series of photos of Sgt Marian Kordasiewicz with AA930 UZ-P at Northolt in the summer of 1942. He is accompanied by F/Sgt Wawrzyniec Jasiński (seated on the tailplane) in photo [154]. During 1942 it became typical for the unit to apply the Polish national marking on the nose and the squadron emblem (the 'Toruń Duck') below the windscreen. Kordasiewicz flew two sorties during 'Jubilee', both in Spitfire VB AR336 UZ-O.

[155]: F/O Jan Kurowski flew AA930 during the midday cover for smoke-laying Blenheims.

[156]: P/O Jerzy Polak was the pilot of AA930 during the early morning patrol. He was the regular pilot of the Spitfire, flying it on about 50 occasions between early May and late September, including the unfortunate last sortie of the aeroplane with No. 306 Sqn.

[157]: AA930 UZ-P in a sorry state at RAF Croydon following P/O Polak's emergency landing in poor visibility on 28 September 1942. His landing run ended in a collision with a car parked at the dispersal point.

154

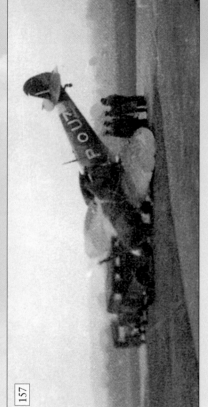

157

156

155

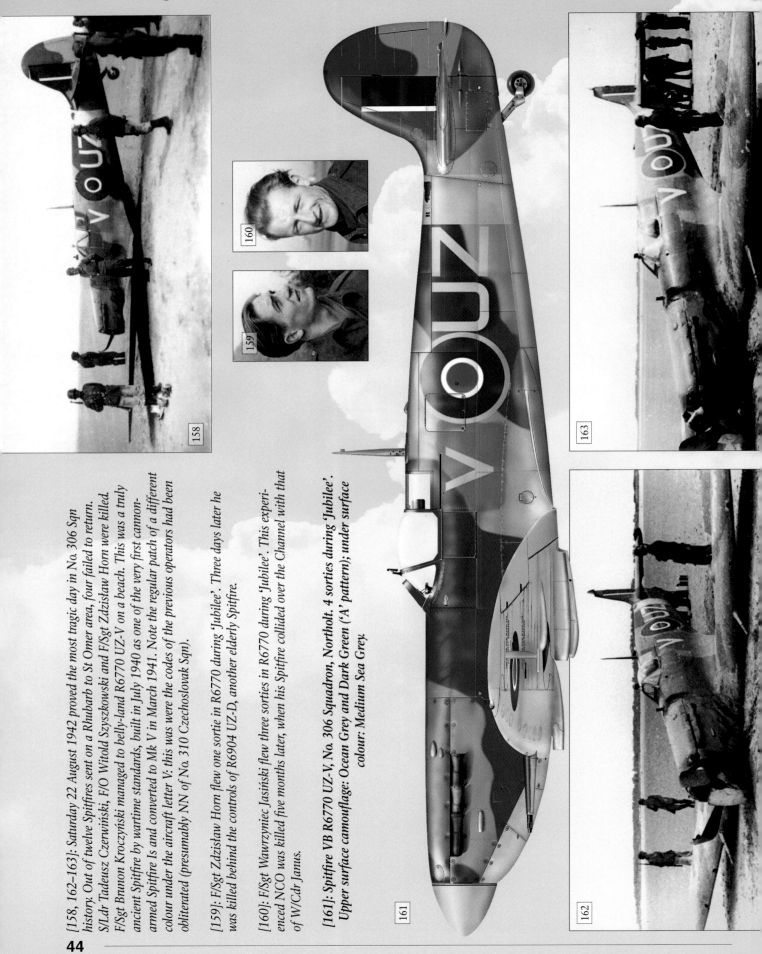

[158, 162–163]: Saturday 22 August 1942 proved the most tragic day in No. 306 Sqn history. Out of twelve Spitfires sent on a Rhubarb to St Omer area, four failed to return. S/Ldr Tadeusz Czerwiński, F/O Witold Szyszkowski and F/Sgt Zdzisław Horn were killed. F/Sgt Brunon Kroczyński managed to belly-land R6770 UZ-V on a beach. This was a truly ancient Spitfire by wartime standards, built in July 1940 as one of the very first cannon-armed Spitfire Is and converted to Mk V in March 1941. Note the regular patch of a different colour under the aircraft letter V: this was were the codes of the previous operators had been obliterated (presumably NN of No. 310 Czechoslovak Sqn).

[159]: F/Sgt Zdzisław Horn flew one sortie in R6770 during 'Jubilee'. Three days later he was killed behind the controls of R6904 UZ-D, another elderly Spitfire.

[160]: F/Sgt Wawrzyniec Jasiński flew three sorties in R6770 during 'Jubilee'. This experienced NCO was killed five months later, when his Spitfire collided over the Channel with that of W/Cdr Janus.

[161]: Spitfire VB R6770 UZ-V, No. 306 Squadron, Northolt. 4 sorties during 'Jubilee'. Upper surface camouflage: Ocean Grey and Dark Green ('A' pattern); under surface colour: Medium Sea Grey.

44

No. 302 Squadron (RAF Heston)

No. 302 was based at the satellite airfield at Heston since early May 1942.

It was commanded by S/Ldr Julian Kowalski, with F/Lts Stanisław Łapka and Marian Chełmecki as flight command- ers. F/Lts Stanisław Chałupa and Piotr Ostaszewski were the Ops Room controllers.

The squadron had an uneventful 'Jubilee': four missions, during which no victories were claimed or losses reported, plus an ASR patrol called back soon after taking off.

[164]: *S/Ldr Julian Kowalski was nicknamed 'Roch Kowalski' after a character from 'Potop' ('Deluge'), a very popular Polish novel by Nobel Prize winner Henryk Sienkiewicz. Kowalski had served with No. 302 Squadron since the Battle of Britain, rising from a Pilot Officer to Squadron Leader, and was virtually tour expired at the time of 'Jubilee', so he only flew one sortie that day.*

[165]: *F/Lt Stanisław Łapka, No. 302 Squadron 'A' Flight Commander, poses with Spitfire VB EN865 WX-L, which he flew twice during 'Jubilee'. A week later he succeeded S/Ldr Kowalski at the head of the squadron.*

[166]: *'B' Flight Commander F/Lt Marian Chełmecki, probably in the cockpit of EN861 WX-N, in which flew two sorties during 'Jubilee'.*

[167]: *One of No. 302 Sqn pilots during 'Jubilee', F/O Tadeusz Ciastuła, went on to become a leading helicopter designer in Britain after the war: his work commenced with the Saro Skeeter and culminated in the Westland Lynx.*

168

169

[168]: EN865 WX-L was the personal mount of S/Ldr Kowalski, and then S/Ldr Łapka. Both this photo and the colour shot [165] were taken in September 1942 at Heston.

[169]: Sgt Hipolit Mikusek in the cockpit of AA854 WX-G, in which he flew two sorties during 'Jubilee'. On 8 September 1942 the same pilot was downed by Focke-Wulfs in this machine, ending up in captivity. The colours and the pattern of the camouflage are a mystery: they certainly do not follow known Fighter Command regulations of the time.

[170]: Unrecognised ground crew work on the machine gun of BM648 WX-R. The Spitfire completed three sorties during 'Jubilee' in the hands of three pilots: F/O Tadeusz Kwiatkowski, P/O Marian Rytka and F/O Eugeniusz Ebenrytter. This photograph was taken in late 1942 or early 1943, after the aeroplane had been completely repainted. The personal name applied diagonally in ornamental style forward of the windscreen has proved impossible to decipher positively, even though several photos of the aeroplane in this guise exist. It may have read Baśka, Janka, Kaśka or Wańka.

170

[171]: *EN922 WX-U undergoing maintenance at Heston in September 1942. The Spitfire completed four sorties during 'Jubilee',
flown alternately by Sgt Adam Tiahnybok and F/O Kazimierz Sporny.*

[172]: *Another unrecognised ground crew member of No. 302 Sqn. The Spitfire is BM651 WX-D, flown twice each by
F/Os Zbigniew Wróblewski and Alojzy Rodziewicz during 'Jubilee'. This photo was taken in late 1942 or early 1943, after the
unit started to apply its badge on the aeroplanes.*

[173]: *One of the most publicised Spitfire VBs of No. 302 Sqn: W3902 WX-T taxies out for take-off from Heston in September
1942 (compare PW 29, pp. 21–24). The aeroplane logged a mere 20 minutes flying time during 'Jubilee', flown by F/O Eugeniusz
Ebenrytter during a cancelled ASR patrol at dawn.*

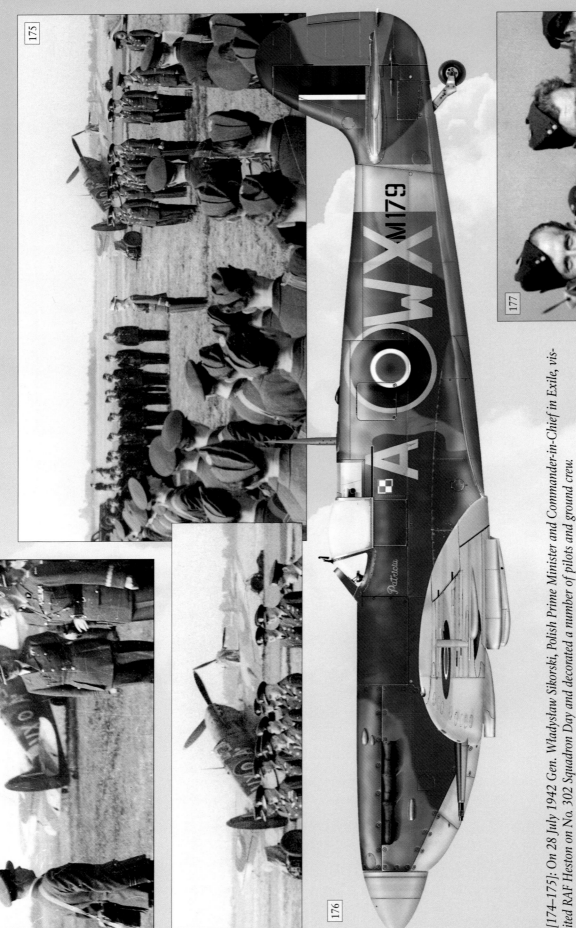

[174-175]: On 28 July 1942 Gen. Wladyslaw Sikorski, Polish Prime Minister and Commander-in-Chief in Exile, visited RAF Heston on No. 302 Squadron Day and decorated a number of pilots and ground crew.

[174]: S/Ldr Julian Kowalski reports to the General on his arrival.

[175]: The guest speaks to members of Nos. 302 and 316 Squadrons based there at the time. Spitfire VB BM179 WX-A can be seen in the background.

[176]: Spitfire VB BM179 WX-A, No. 302 Squadron, Heston. 2 sorties during 'Jubilee'. Upper surface camouflage: Ocean Grey and Dark Green ('A' pattern); under surface colour: Medium Sea Grey. Polish squares both sides of the fuselage near the cockpit. 'Patricia' personal name applied forward of the cockpit, port side only.

[177]: Two ground crew members pose with the decorations they have just received: Cpl Stanisław Liguziński (left) with the Krzyż Walecznych (Cross of Valour) and F/Sgt Józef Gołębiowski with the Srebrny Krzyż Zasługi (Silver Cross of Merit). BM179 WX-A can be seen in the distance, note the peculiar patch of dark colour beneath the code letter A.

[178]: Anonymous NCOs posing with the same Spitfire. BM179 had been used by No. 501 Sqn RAF before delivery to No. 302. The patch of green beneath the A is where their SD code was overpainted. It is not known if 'Patricia' was applied in No. 302 Sqn, or dated back to No. 501 service.

[179]: A group of No. 302 Sqn 'A' Flight pilots photographed by the side of BM179 in the summer of 1942. Left to right: F/O Mieczysław Gorzula, P/O Jerzy Urbański (who flew this Spitfire during one of his two 'Jubilee' sorties), probably F/O Alojzy Rodziewicz, F/O Zbigniew Wróblewski, F/Lt Stanisław Łapka, F/O Kazimierz Sporny, P/O Andrzej Beyer, probably Sgt Eustachy Łucyszyn, F/O Tadeusz Ciastuła and F/O Władysław Kamiński. Note the suitably marked cloth covering over the engine and another one over the cockpit glazing.

181

180

183

[180]: W3954 WX-B at readiness, with the ground power supply plugged in. LAC Roman Rogalski is seated on the wing.

[181]: P/O Andrzej Beyer in the cockpit of the Spitfire.

[182]: Sgt Eustachy Łucyszyn, F/Sgt Kazimierz Kobusiński and Sgt Kazimierz Benziński at Heston in late 1942. Benziński flew two sorties in W3954 WX-B during 'Jubilee', Kobusiński two in AD317 WX-K.

[183]: Spitfire VB W3954 WX-B, No. 302 Squadron, Heston. 2 sorties during 'Jubilee'. Upper surface camouflage: unspecified dark grey and Dark Green ('A' pattern); under surface colour: Medium Sea Grey. Polish squares both sides of the fuselage near the cockpit.

182

[184, 186–187]: A series of photos taken during engine tests of AD317 WX-K at Croydon in July 1942. It is noteworthy that it was still fitted with the early style Rotol propeller, with narrow root blades and blunt spinner, usually associated with the Spitfire II rather than V, but in fact seen on many early CBAF-built Spitfire Vs.

[185]: Spitfire VB AD317 WX-K, No. 302 Squadron, Heston. 3 sorties during 'Jubilee'. Upper surface camouflage: Ocean Grey and Dark Green ('A' pattern); under surface colour: Medium Sea Grey.

No. 308 Squadron (RAF Heston)

At the time of 'Jubilee', No. 308 was the most recent arrival in the 1st Wing, having moved to Heston at the end of July 1942.

The squadron was commanded by S/Ldr Walerian Żak, with F/Lt Tadeusz Koc and Jerzy Popławski as flight commanders. Ops Room controller duties were performed by F/Lts Wieńczysław Barański and Mieczysław Sulerzycki.

Similar to No. 302, No. 308 Sqn flew four uneventful missions that day, with no victories or casualties.

[188]: *No. 308 Sqn pilots at Hutton Cranswick in July 1942, before the move to Heston. Left to right: F/O Adam Habela, F/O Karol Marschall, F/O Bronisław Mach, P/O Stanisław Madej, Sgt Jan Osoba, F/O Józef Sobolewski, F/O Zbigniew Kobierzycki, F/O Tadeusz Stabrowski, Sgt Feliks Marek, F/Lt Jerzy Popławski, S/Ldr Walerian Żak, F/Lt Tadeusz Koc, F/O Stanisław Wandzilak, F/O Julian Żuromski, P/O Tadeusz Schiele, Sgt Jan Okrój, P/O Marian Kotlarz, Sgt Stanisław Domański, Sgt Wacław Korwel and Sgt Tadeusz Turek. Jumbie, the squadron mascot, is seated on the propeller spinner. The Spitfire is presumably S/Ldr Żak's personal mount, BL239 ZF-Q, in which he flew three sorties during 'Jubilee'.*

[189]: *Photos of No. 308 Sqn Spitfires from 1941 and 1942 are extremely rare, unfortunately. This image, taken on 24 June 1942 at Hutton Cranswick during the Squadron Day celebrations, shows W/Cdr Tadeusz Rolski (saluting) and S/Ldr Walerian Żak, with Spitfire V ZF-A in the background. This was most probably BL977, which was flown twice during 'Jubilee' by F/Lt Tadeusz Koc. Note that at the time it still displayed No. 308 Squadron's oversize Polish national marking below the rearmost exhaust section.*

[190]: *Spitfire VB BL412 ZF-C at RAF Heston about the time of 'Jubilee'. The aeroplane completed three sorties on 19 August 1942, one each by S/Ldr Tadeusz Nowierski (the Deputy Wing Leader), P/O Stanisław Madej and Sgt Tadeusz Turek. By the time this photo was taken the Polish marking on No. 308 Sqn Spitfires had been reapplied in small size immediately aft of the propeller. Five pilots in the photo have been identified: standing on the ground, left to right, are F/Lt Tadeusz Koc, P/O Marian Kotlarz and F/O Jan Jakubowski; F/O Bolesław Palej is standing on the wing and P/O Donat Mickiewicz is seated on the cockpit door.*

[191–193] *An anonymous fitter, F/O Tadeusz Stabrowski and his personal Spitfire VB ZF-Y, presumably AB273, the aeroplane Stabrowski flew twice during 'Jubilee'. The aircraft letter Y on the bottom cowling, probably in yellow, can just be made out. The Spitfire featured the 'Drunken Angel' personal emblem on both sides near the windscreen. Photos of a number of personal emblems on No. 308 Sqn Spitfire VBs are known, but few can be linked to specific aircraft.*

[194] *Confusingly, the '308' numberplate was shared by two Spitfire squadrons participating in 'Jubilee': the Polish one and the 308th Fighter Squadron of the 31st Fighter Group USAAF. The American unit saw its combat debut over Dieppe on 19 August 1942. Here, pilots of 'B' Flight of the 308th FS pose at RAF Westhampnett in September 1942. Left to right: Lt. Charles Van Reed, Lt. Mathew Mosby, Capt. Adrian Davis, Lt. E. G. Johnson, Lt. Derwood Smith, Lt. Westley Ballard, Lt. John Ramer and Capt. Frank Hill.*

[195] *The 308th FS used code letters HL. This early CBAF-built Spitfire VB (note the early-style Rotol propeller with narrow-root blades and blunt spinner, and the tear-drop fairing on the side of the cowling immediately aft of the prop) was often flown by Capt. Frank Hill in the summer 1942. During 'Jubilee', he claimed the first victory for the 308th FS, a Focke-Wulf 190 probably destroyed, although it is not known if he flew this Spitfire on that occasion.*

197

196

[196–197]: BL940 ZF-V in the early summer of 1942, showing one of the usual pilots of the Spitfire, F/O Stanisław Wandzilak (wearing a Mae-West) with two unrecognised fitters. Note the style of the aircraft letter on the lower cowling.

199

198

[198–199]: Other ground crew members photographed with the same Spitfire in late summer or autumn of 1942. By that time the had been fitted with the Malcolm hood. There was also some repainting around the bottom of the letter Z. These are orthochromatic photos, and the badge of No. 308 Sqn is not well visible, since the yellow 'Winged Arrow' motif is rendered rather dark, blending in with its black diamond background. For the same reason the outer ring of the fuselage roundel is virtually indiscernible from the blue one.

[200]: Spitfire VB BL940 ZF-V, No. 308 Squadron, Heston. 1 sortie during 'Jubilee'. Upper surface camouflage: Ocean Grey and Dark Green ('A' pattern); under surface colour: Medium Sea Grey. Polish squares both sides of the nose. No. 308 Sqn badge below the windscreen on both sides of the fuselage.

[201]: Another trio of ground crew members on BL940 ZF-V in the second half of 1942. The framing of the Malcolm hood appears still unpainted.

[202]: F/Sgt Władysław Majchrzyk flew three sorties on 19 August 1942, but only one of these in BL940, even though this was his usual mount, shared with F/O Wandzilak.

55

[203]: F/O Bolesław Palej completed three sorties in BM538 ZF-R during 'Jubilee'.

[204]: Spitfire VB BM538 ZF-R, No. 308 Squadron, Heston. 3 sorties during 'Jubilee'. Upper surface camouflage: Ocean Grey and Dark Green ('A' pattern); under surface colour: Medium Sea Grey. Polish squares both sides of the nose.

[205]: BM538 ZF-R with ground crew members who have, sadly, not been recognised.

[206]: W/O Kazimierz Konopka in front of a Spitfire VB ZF-R, possibly BM538, at Northolt in late 1942. Born in 1899, Konopka was deemed too old for operational service in the exiled Polish AF. Instead, he flew as a ferry and test pilot with a number of maintenance units. In late May 1942 (roughly half a year before this photo was taken) he ferried BM538 from No. 30 Satellite Landing Ground at Brockton (following a few weeks of storage of the brand new Spitfire there) to No. 9 MU at Cosford, where it was then prepared for delivery to No. 308 Sqn

No. 303 Squadron (RAF Redhill)

Without a doubt the most famous Polish squadron, No. 303, was resting in the 2nd Wing at RAF Kirton-in-Lindsey since mid-June 1942. It deployed to Redhill on 15 August, to reinforce the 1st Wing for 'Jubilee'.

It was commanded by S/Ldr Jan Zumbach, with F/Lts Zygmunt Bieńkowski and Janusz Marciniak as flight commanders. F/Lts Władysław Gnyś and Jerzy Palusiński were the Ops Room controllers.

No. 303 emerged as the top-scoring Fighter Command squadron during 'Jubilee', with seven and two shared German aircraft destroyed to their credit, claimed during three of their four missions. Notably, they had a lazy morning, unlike every other squadron of the 1st Wing, as their first take-off did not take place until 9.30 a.m.

Three of their Spitfires were damaged in air combats: BL567 RF-T of Sgt Józef Karczmarz in the morning, EN912 RF-M of F/O Longin Majewski during the midday mission, and AR366 RF-C of Sgt Aleksander Rokitnicki in the afternoon. Tragically, the latter mission also saw the death of P/O Adam Damm, shot down into the Channel in BL574 RF-F.

[207]: *One of a series of colour photos of No. 303 Squadron members with Spitfire VB BL670 RF-K, probably taken in June 1942, before the unit departed Northolt for a period of rest. Standing on the ground, right to left: F/Lt Zygmunt Bieńkowski ('A' Flight Commander), S/Ldr Jan Zumbach, F/Lt Janusz Marciniak ('B' Flight Commander) and F/O Eugeniusz Horbaczewski. F/O Longin Majewski is seated on the open cockpit door and Sgt Arkadiusz Bondarczuk sits on the wing next to Horbaczewski.*

[208]: *Another photo from the same session: a group walks away from the Spitfire. Left to right: F/Lt Janusz Marciniak, Sgt Ryszard Górecki, F/O Antoni Kolubiński, F/O Jerzy Schmidt, F/Sgt Kazimierz Wünsche, Sgt Józef Stasik, S/Ldr Jan Zumbach, Sgt Arkadiusz Bondarczuk, F/O Longin Majewski, F/O Zbigniew Zarębski, u/i mechanic, F/Sgt Wacław Giermer, u/i (obscured), P/O Tadeusz Kołecki, P/O Stanisław Socha, P/O Adam Damm. Note their bright red silk scarves, standard in No. 303. Each of the Polish fighter squadrons had these in a particular colour or pattern.*

[209–210]: *A series of air-to-air shots of six No. 303 Sqn Spitfires were taken in the first half of August 1942 as publicity images for the forthcoming celebrations of the Squadron Day (1 September). The formation included BM144 RF-D, AR371 RF-B (see pp. 68–69), BL567 RF-T (p. 67), BL594 RF-G, AB183 RF-A (pp. 70–71) and BM540 RF-I. The latter's code letter was expanded into a girl's name (possibly 'Irka'), which in most photos makes it look like an L rather than I. It was flown by F/Sgt Wacław Giermer on 19 August over Dieppe. In two sorties, he was credited with a Focke-Wulf 190 probably destroyed and a Heinkel 111 shared destroyed.*

[211]: *Soon after that session S/Ldr Zumbach chose EP594 as his new personal mount (see pp. 62–63) and BM144 was taken over by F/Lt Bieńkowski (see pp. 64–65). This photo, taken during one of numerous Zumbach's visits from Kirton-in-Lindsey to Northolt before and after 'Jubilee', probably shows him with EP594 RF-D. Note the message on the rudder: another case of chalked 'air mail' between Polish Spitfire squadrons.*

[212]: *Pilots of No. 303 Sqn in front of the Officers' Mess at Redhill (the requisitioned Barn Ridge House) prior to 'Jubilee'. Standing, left to right: probably P/O Adam Damm, P/O Antoni Głowacki and F/Lt Janusz Marciniak. Seated, left to right: F/O Longin Majewski (by the column), unrecognised (in front of him), F/O Eugeniusz Horbaczewski and P/O Czesław Mroczyk.*

[213]: At Redhill No. 303 Squadron replaced No. 611 Squadron RAF, whose trophies can be seen by the side of the hut: panels from a Ju 88 (with the swastika) and a Do 215 (with the black cross).

[214]: S/Ldr Zumbach looks into the camera, seated behind him are P/O Adam Damm, P/O Zbigniew Wojda and probably P/O Mirosław Szelestowski. Note the '611 AUXILIARY SQUADRON' label near the door.

[215]: P/O Adam Damm on the ground, F/Sgt Kazimierz Wünsche and P/O Czesław Mroczyk sit on the stairs, F/O Eugeniusz Horbaczewski is leaving the hut, others crowding inside.

[216]: Left to right: Sgt Alojzy Rutecki, F/Sgt Kazimierz Wünsche, P/O Stanisław Socha, P/O Czesław Mroczyk.

[217]: No. 303 Sqn pilots watch something anxiously in front of the dispersal hut at Redhill. Left to right: P/O Antoni Głowacki, F/O Longin Majewski, F/Sgt Mieczysław Adamek, Sgt Józef Stasik and Sgt Arkadiusz Bondarczuk.

[218–221]: No. 303 Squadron pilots have a meal at Redhill. Participants of the squadron's first operation, flown between 9.30 and 11.30, are all wearing their Mae-Wests, in anticipation of their mission, so this is probably their breakfast.

[218]: Left to right: Sgt Stanisław Górny, Sgt Włodzimierz Chojnacki, F/Sgt Kazimierz Wünsche, Sgt Arkadiusz Bondarczuk, Sgt Aleksander Rokitnicki, P/O Czesław Mroczyk, unrecognised WAAF, F/Lt Zygmunt Bieńkowski and F/Sgt Wacław Giermer.

[219]: Left to right: F/O Antoni Kolubiński, probably Sgt Józef Karczmarz, P/O Czesław Mroczyk, unrecognised, the WAAF, two unrecognised, S/Ldr Jan Zumbach and P/O Stefan Baran.

[220]: Left to right: probably F/O Antoni Kolubiński (with his back to the camera), F/O Longin Majewski, S/Ldr Jan Zumbach, probably F/Sgt Jan Palak.

[221]: Left to right: P/O Czesław Mroczyk, unrecognised, F/Sgt Kazimierz Wünsche, F/Lt Zygmunt Bieńkowski, S/Ldr Jan Zumbach and F/Sgt Wacław Giermer.

[222]: *Probably the same meal. Right to left: Sgt Ryszard Górecki, F/Sgt Mieczysław Popek, probably P/O Adam Damm, P/O Tadeusz Kołecki, Sgt Mieczysław Adamek, Sgt Józef Stasik, unrecognised (with his back to the camera). S/Ldr Jan Zumbach's Spitfire VB EP594 RF-D can be seen in the background.*

[223]: *Same location, another meal. Seated on the ground in the foreground, left to right: P/Os Stanisław Socha, Adam Damm, Tadeusz Kołecki and Czesław Mroczyk. EP594 RF-D can be seen in the background again.*

[224]: Fitting Zumbach's trade-mark taller rear-view mirror on his new Spitfire: EP594, in mid-August 1942. The squadron emblem and the pilot's scoreboard have already been applied below the windscreen.

[225]: P/O Stanisław Socha posing with EP594 RF-D at Redhill. The scoreboard under the windscreen shows eleven confirmed victories, as yet lacking those scored by Zumbach in this Spitfire over Dieppe.

[226]: Spitfire VB EP594 RF-D, No. 303 Squadron, Redhill. 2 sorties and 1 ⅓-1-0 victories during 'Jubilee'. Upper surface camouflage: Ocean Grey and Dark Green ('A' pattern); under surface colour: Medium Sea Grey. Polish squares both sides of the nose. No. 303 Sqn badge below the windscreen on both sides of the fuselage. The score of S/Ldr Jan Zumbach marked in form of black crosses below the squadron badge. 'Donald Duck' personal emblem applied forward of the cockpit, port side only.

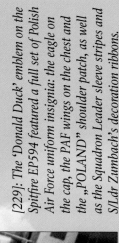

[229]: The 'Donald Duck' emblem on the Spitfire EP594 featured a full set of Polish Air Force uniform insignia: the eagle on the cap, the PAF wings on the chest and the „POLAND" shoulder patch, as well as the Squadron Leader sleeve stripes and S/Ldr Zumbach's decoration ribbons.

[227]: S/Ldr Jan Zumbach in the cockpit of his Spitfire VB EP594 RF-D, probably on 27 or 28 August 1942, when photographs were taken for use in press releases to be published on 1 September, No. 303 Squadron Day. The squadron emblem and the scoreboard are clearly visible below the windscreen, with the pilot's 'Donald Duck' personal emblem further forward. The black crosses include those applied after 'Jubilee', when Zumbach's score stood at twelve and one shared Luftwaffe aircraft destroyed (two rows of black crosses with white outlines), four probably destroyed (crosses with red outlines) and one damaged (a cross without outline). See 'Polish Wings' 29, pp. 58–60 for more details.

[228]: Holy mass celebrated in a hangar at Kirton-in-Lindsey on 1 September 1942, No. 303 Squadron Day. Mr Władysław Raczkiewicz, the Polish President in Exile, is seated in the centre, with his ADC standing behind him. EP594 RF-D can be seen in the foreground, with AB183 RF-A flanking the altar on the other side.

[231]

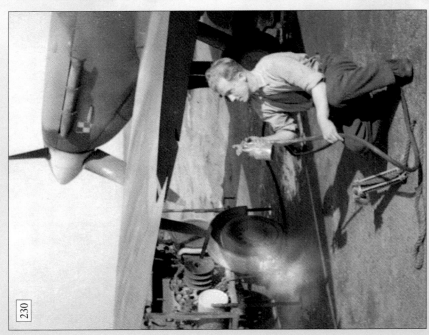

[230]

[232]

[230–232]: *Spitfire VB BM144 RF-D was last flown by S/Ldr Zumbach on 11 August 1942. Two days later F/Lt Bieńkowski flew it as for the first time, presumably as RF-H. Subsequently, the Spitfire was re-finished with a new coat of camouflage, but the markings were generally retained as they were (the original 'A'/'A1' roundel and fin flash still show through the late 'C'/'C1' ones). The code letters and other markings were then retouched, and the aircraft letter was expanded into the name of Bieńkowski's fiancée Halszka (Halina) Grzybowska.*

[233]: *No. 303 Squadron Spitfires in flight over England in late September 1942: BM144 RF-H, AB183 RF-A, W3893 RF-U and BL567 RF-T. W3893 was the personal mount of F/Lt Janusz Marciniak, commanding 'B' Flight, who flew it when he claimed a Focke-Wulf 190 probably destroyed during 'Jubilee'.*

234

[234]: Spitfire VB BM144 RF-H, No. 303 Squadron, Redhill. 2 sorties during 'Jubilee'. Upper surface camouflage: Ocean Grey and Dark Green ('A' pattern); under surface colour: Medium Sea Grey. Polish squares both sides of the nose. No. 303 Sqn badge below the windscreen on both sides of the fuselage. 'Halszka' personal name applied as an extension of the aircraft letter on both sides of the fuselage.

[235]: Starting up BM144 RF H in early 1943. The wing tips had been clipped by then but this did not mean it was modified to the LF.V standard.

[236]: An air-to-air portrait of BM144 RF H on 17 May 1943, when No. 303 Sqn escorted Gen. Montgomery's aeroplane on his return trip to London following the victorious North African campaign. By that time the serial number of the Spitfire had been re-applied in small, two-inch characters at the top of the Sky band.

235

[237]: BL574 RF-F at Redhill, in the background. No. 303 Sqn pilots and ground crew gather around S/Ldr Zumbach (his distinctive hairdo can just be made out in the middle of the group, behind the forage cap of the officer in the foreground). Sgt Włodzimierz Chojnacki in his Mae-West faces the camera.

[238]: BL574 had preceded BM144 as F/Lt Bieńkowski's personal RF-H. This is the only known photo of it in that guise, in the background of an image taken at Northolt in mid-1942.

[239]: Sgt Józef Stasik flew BL574 RF-F during his first sortie, when he was credited with a Focke-Wulf destroyed. Born on 15 February 1921, Stasik was the youngest Polish pilot to participate in 'Jubilee'. This portrait photo has proved so good that doctored versions, with Stasik's face replaced by another one, have also been seen in print!

[240]: P/O Adam Damm flew BL574 RF-F during the afternoon convoy patrol when he was shot down into the Channel and killed.

[241]: Spitfire VB BL574 RF-F, No. 303 Squadron, Redhill. 2 sorties and 1-0-0 victories during 'Jubilee', shot down in combat. Upper surface camouflage: Ocean Grey and Dark Green ('A' pattern); under surface colour: Medium Sea Grey. Polish squares both sides of the nose. No. 303 Sqn badge below the windscreen on both sides of the fuselage.

[242–243] Spitfire VB BL567 RF-T in photos from the early August air-to-air session, accompanied by AR371 RF-B and other aircraft. BL567 completed just one sortie during 'Jubilee', suffering light damage that prevented it from flying any more that day. No details are known regarding the circumstances or scope of the damage, but the aircraft was repaired within days.

[244] Sgt Józef Karczmarz was the pilot of BL567 RF-T during the morning mission, claiming a Focke-Wulf 190 probably destroyed.

[245] Spitfire VB BL567 RF-T, No. 303 Squadron, Redhill. 1 sortie and 0-1-0 victories during 'Jubilee', damaged in combat. Upper surface camouflage: Ocean Grey and Dark Green ('A' pattern); under surface colour: Medium Sea Grey. Polish squares both sides of the nose. No. 303 Sqn badge below the windscreen on both sides of the fuselage.

[246]: AR371 RF-B in the formation during the early August session.

[247]: Spitfire VB AR371 RF-B, No. 303 Squadron, Redhill. 2 sorties during 'Jubilee'. Upper surface camouflage: Ocean Grey and Dark Green ('A' pattern); under surface colour: Medium Sea Grey. Polish squares both sides of the nose. No. 303 Sqn badge below the windscreen on both sides of the fuselage.

[248]: During July and August No. 303 Squadron shared RAF Kirton-in-Lindsey with the P-38-equipped 94th Fighter Squadron 1st Fighter Group USAAF, helping the American pilots learn the basics of fighter operations in the ETO. Here, one of the Lightnings flies above three Spitfire VBs of No. 303 Sqn: AR371 RF-B, AA913 RF-P and AB183 RF-A. All three participated in 'Jubilee'.

[249-251]: A series of photos of Sgt Józef Stasik in the cockpit of AR371 RF-B at Kirton-in-Lindsey in August 1942. Note his reflection in the rear-view mirror!

[252]: A trio of ground crew servicing a Spitfire VB at Kirton-in-Lindsey in August 1942. The inscription on the nose might suggest that this is AR371, in line with the squadron's tradition of applying girl's names to match the aircraft letter. However, the name was applied on the nose rather than rear fuselage, and possibly in chalk not paint, so it may have had nothing to do with the aircraft letter.

250

252

249

251

[253]: Spitfire VB AB183 RF-A, No. 303 Squadron, Redhill. 3 sorties and 1-0-0 victories during 'Jubilee'. Upper surface camouflage: unspecified dark grey and Dark Green ('A' pattern); under surface colour: Medium Sea Grey. Polish squares both sides of the nose. No. 303 Sqn badge below the windscreen on both sides of the fuselage.

256

257

258

[254–255]: More formation shots from the photo session in the first half of August 1942 that featured BM144 RF-D, AR371 RF-B, BL567 RF-T, BL594 RF-G, AB183 RF-A and BM540 RF-I. Note the prominent traces of overpainted large early roundels on the under side of AB183's wing.

[256]: BM144 RF-D (the 'Donald Duck' just visible forward of the 'Kościuszko badge' disc) leads AB183 RF-A and AR371 RF-B to take off from Kirton-in-Lindsey in August 1942 for the photo session. Note the overall darker appearance of AB183 compared to the other two and how the nominal Ocean Grey areas of its camouflage appear darker than the Dark Green ones.

[257]: AB183 RF-A photographed in early 1943. The rudder had been replaced and/or repainted by then, with prominent contrast of the regulation camouflage tones (and a different colour division line).

[258]: P/O Tadeusz Kołecki flew AB183 RF-A during the morning mission when he scored a Junkers 88 destroyed.

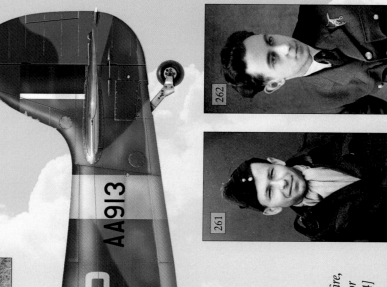

[259]: A mobile canteen provides a welcome break to No. 303 Sqn ground crew; Sgt Karol Blachuta first left. The Spitfire on the right is AA913 RF-P.

[260]: Spitfire VB AA913 RF-P, No. 303 Squadron, Redhill. 4 sorties during 'Jubilee'. Upper surface camouflage: Ocean Grey and Dark Green ('A' pattern); under surface colour: Medium Sea Grey. Polish squares both sides of the nose. No. 303 Sqn badge below the windscreen on both sides of the fuselage.

[261]: F/Sgt Jan Palak flew AA913 RF-P during No. 303 Sqn's first and third mission on 19 August.

[262]: P/O Zbigniew Wojda flew AA913 RF-P during the second and fourth missions of No. 303 Sqn that day.

[263–266]: A series of publicity photos of Sgt Arkadiusz Bondarczuk with AA913 RF-P. In fact he did not normally fly this Spitfire, as he was a pilot of 'A' Flight (which used aircraft coded RF-A to -L). He flew two sorties during 'Jubilee', one in BL594 RF-G (or possibly AR366 RF-C, see footnote on p. 90), and the other in AR318 RF-L. Note AB183 RF-A in the background of photos [264] and [265].

266

264

263

265

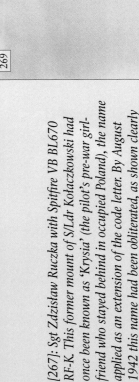

[267]: *Sgt Zdzisław Ruczka with Spitfire VB BL670 RF-K. This former mount of S/Ldr Kołaczkowski had once been known as 'Krysia' (the pilot's pre-war girl-friend who stayed behind in occupied Poland), the name applied as an extension of the code letter. By August 1942 this name had been obliterated, as shown clearly in this photo.*

[268]: *F/Sgts Kazimierz Wünsche (left) and Mieczysław Popek pose by the side of BL670 RF-K. During the mid-day mission Popek flew the Spitfire when he claimed a Focke-Wulf shared destroyed.*

[269–270]: *P/O Stanisław Socha with BL670 RF-K, in which he was credited with a Focke-Wulf 190 and a Junkers 88 destroyed during 'Jubilee'. The name 'Wojtek' (a diminutive form of Kołaczkowski's first name) in hand-script style on the cowling was retained, as was the presentation name 'EVER READY II' (see PW29, pp. 43–46 for more details regarding this Spitfire).*

[271]: *Spitfire VB BL670 RF-K, No. 303 Squadron, Redhill. 2 sorties and 2½-0-0 victories during 'Jubilee'. Upper surface camouflage: Ocean Grey and Dark Green ('A' pattern); under surface colour: Medium Sea Grey. Polish squares both sides of the nose. No. 303 Sqn badge below the windscreen on both sides of the fuselage. 'Wojtek' personal name applied on both sides of the engine cowling.*

[272]: *Spitfire VB AR366 RF-C, No. 303 Squadron, Redhill. 2 sorties and 1⅓-0-0 victories during 'Jubilee', seriously damaged in combat. Upper surface camouflage: Ocean Grey and Dark Green ('A' pattern); under surface colour: Medium Sea Grey. Polish squares both sides of the nose. No. 303 Sqn badge below the windscreen on both sides of the fuselage.*

[273–274]: Sgt Aleksander Rokitnicki in his Mae-West by Spitfire VB AR366 RF-C. According to the ORB of No. 303 Sqn, F/O Horbaczewski used the Spitfire to score a Focke-Wulf destroyed. It is not impossible, however, that he flew another Spitfire during that combat (see footnote on p. 90).

[275]: In the afternoon Sgt Rokitnicki definitely flew AR366 RF-C when he was credited with a Heinkel 111 shared destroyed. The Spitfire was badly shot up during that sortie and Rokitnicki barely made it back. Here, P/O Stanisław Socha inspects the damage.

[276–277]: Close-up photos showing damage to the tail of AR366. Note also the rudder guard on the bottom of the rear fuselage, used on Spitfires employed for target towing.

[280]

[282]

[281]

[279]

[278]

[278]: F/Sgt Mieczysław Adamek flew two sorties during 'Jubilee', using his personalised Spitfire VB, BL748 RF-W, but failed to score that day.

[279]: Sgt Włodzimierz Chojnacki also flew two sorties in the same Spitfire that day.

[280–282, 284]: A sequence of photos showing BL748 at Kirton-in-Lindsey in August 1942. The unrecognised 'erk' seated on the wing root is handling the camera gun, an essential item of fighters at the time. Personal combat reports filed following air combats normally ended '… Camera gun exposed'. This camera was normally fitted inside the wing, looking through a port in the leading edge. It operated when the pilot fired his guns and filmed the area ahead of the aeroplane, roughly where armament was aiming, to record any hits scored at the target.

[283]: Spitfire VB BL748 RF-W, No. 303 Squadron, Redhill. 4 sorties during 'Jubilee'. Upper surface camouflage: Ocean Grey and Dark Green ('A' pattern); under surface colour: Medium Sea Grey. Polish squares both sides of the nose. No 303 Sqn badge below the windscreen on both sides of the fuselage. The score of F/Sgt Mieczysław Adamek marked in form of black crosses below the squadron badge.

[284]: During 1941-1943 F/Sgt Adamek flew a sequence of RF-W coded Spitfire VBs that displayed his scoreboard. BL748 was the third of these (compare PW29, p. 34) and was adorned with seven black crosses, the significance of which is not clear. Five of these certainly referred to his five confirmed victories scored in service with No. 303 Sqn. The other two may have either denoted his two shared confirmed 'kills' over Poland in 1939, or two other victories in No. 303 Sqn service: a probable and a Messerschmitt 109 destroyed on the ground.

285

288

287

286

[285]: *Spitfire VB BM531 RF-V before No. 303 Squadron departed Northolt for Kirton-in-Lindsey on 16 June 1942. The fuselage roundel and the fin flash have already been modified to have narrow white and yellow portions (the added area of red showing clearly).*

[286]: *P/O Zbigniew Wojda and an unrecognised ground crew with BM531 RF-V. The line of black crosses can just be made out below the windscreen. Wojda shared this Spitfre with Szelestowski as his usual mount between September and November 1942.*

[287–288]: *F/Lt Jerzy Radomski in the cockpit of Spitfre VB BM531 RF-V in late 1942 or early 1943. The six black crosses denoted the score (five confirmed destroyed and one probable) of F/O Bolesław Gładych who had been the usual pilot of the Spitfire in the spring of 1942 until he left No. 303 Sqn in early July.*

[289]: *P/O Mirosław Szelestowski flew two sorties in BM531 during 'Jubilee'. He was the usual pilot of the Spitfire between July 1942 and June 1943.*

[290]: *Sgt Alojzy Rutecki flew BM531 RF-V during the afternoon mission on 19 August 1942 when he was credited with a Heinkel 111 shared destroyed.*

[291]: *P/O Zbigniew Wojda in the cockpit of BM531 RF-V with the six crosses shown to advantage.*

[292]: *Spitfire VB BM531 RF-V, No. 303 Squadron, Redhill. 3 sorties and ⅓-0-0 victories during 'Jubilee'. Upper surface camouflage: Ocean Grey and Dark Green ('A' pattern); under surface colour: Medium Sea Grey. Polish squares both sides of the nose. No. 303 Sqn badge below the windscreen on both sides of the fuselage. The score of F/O Bolesław Gładych marked in form of black crosses below the squadron badge.*

[293–294]: *BM531 RF-V and other Spitfires of No. 303 Sqn at Kirton-in-Lindsey. Unfortunately, none of the 'erks' has been identified.*

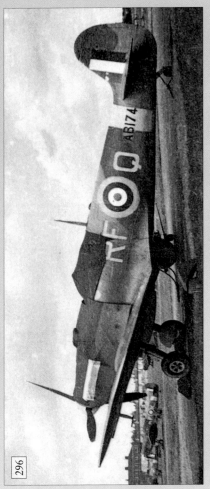

296

295

297

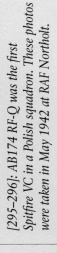

[295–296]: AB174 RF-Q was the first
Spitfire VC in a Polish squadron. These photos
were taken in May 1942 at RAF Northolt.

[297]: An anonymous airman on the Spitfire
photographed after the change of roundel style.
As explained earlier (see BM131 JH-Q on pp.
22–23), Q-coded aircraft were usually called
'kukutka' in Polish squadrons. On AB174 this
Polish word (pronounced 'kookoow-kah') was
jokingly 'transcribed' to English spelling as
QQWCA.

[298]: Between late May and September 1942
AB174 was mostly flown by P/O Antoni
Głowacki (famed for being Poland's only 'ace
in a day', when he was credited with five 'kills'
on 24 August 1940 with No. 501 Sqn RAF).
He poses here on the Spitfire, marked with his
scoreboard. The photo was taken before No. 303
Sqn left Northolt in mid-June. During 'Jubilee'
Głowacki was credited with a Focke-Wulf 190
probably destroyed and a Heinkel 111 shared
destroyed while flying AB174.

[299]: *Three ground crew members photographed with P/O Głowacki's Spitfire VC on the same occasion. Left to right: Cpl Jan Brycki, LAC Antoni Kapciak and Cpl Józef Włodarczyk. The eight black crosses with white outlines denote confirmed victories credited to the pilot by mid-1942. The significance of the other three crosses is unclear, as at the time of these photos he had been credited with two German aircraft probably destroyed and three damaged.*

[300]: *Spitfire VC AB174 RF-Q, No. 303 Squadron, Redhill. 2 sorties and ⅓-1-0 victories during 'Jubilee'. Upper surface camouflage: Ocean Grey and Dark Green ('A' pattern); under surface colour: Medium Sea Grey. Polish squares both sides of the fuselage. The score of P/O Antoni Głowacki marked in form of black crosses below the squadron badge. 'Qgwca' personal name applied as an extension of the aircraft letter on both sides of the fuselage.*

Aftermath

The two top-scoring squadrons did not stay long in the south of England. No. 303 Sqn returned to Kirton-in-Lindsey on 20 August, staying there until the end of January 1943, when it returned for another tour with the 1st Wing. No. 317 Sqn left Northolt on 5 September 1942 for their period of rest. The unit returned to the 1st Wing in June 1943. Nos. 302, 306 and 308 Sqns remained with the 1st Wing into 1943.

W/Cdr Stefan Janus was awarded the Distinguished Service Order and the citation praised his 'great skill and determination when leading his Wing. These fine qualities were amply demonstrated during the Combined Operations at Dieppe on 19th August 1942, when the Wing gained outstanding success and inflicted serious losses on the enemy'. However, he was not able to receive the DSO before the end of the war, as he failed to return from operations before the award was made and spent the rest of the war as a PoW.

Several Polish pilots were awarded the Distinguished Flying Cross or a bar to their DFC.

On a broad scale, the effort of the Western Allies would concentrate in the Mediterranean. Operation 'Torch' in November 1942 paved the way to the defeat of the Axis forces in North Africa in May 1943, followed by the invasions of Sicily in July 1943 and Italy in September 1943. Meanwhile, the balance on the Eastern front has shifted in favour of the Soviets.

In terms of aerial warfare conducted from Britain, 'Jubilee' heralded the entry of US Army Air Force units into the operations over Europe. Their modest beginnings with just three Spitfire squadrons over Dieppe gradually evolved into a grand-scale air offensive into the heart of Germany. This eventually forced the *Luftwaffe* to largely withdraw home. Even if the

claims to fame of the 1st Polish Wing included 'being the first Spitfire Wing to operate over Germany' (as recorded in the RAF Northolt Combat Diary on 12 August 1943), this was an exception rather than rule. The Reich air defence was virtually beyond reach of UK-based Spitfires.

Disappointment with the absence of German aircraft in the air over Western Europe would soon drive many Polish Spitfire pilots to volunteer for service in Africa (see nos. 13 and 30 in the 'Polish Wings' series, by this author). And by the time of the Normandy landings all Polish fighter squadrons had trained in the ground attack role in addition to air-to-air fighter duties.

[301]: On 2 October 1942 at RAF Woodvale, S/Ldr Stanisław Skalski was decorated by ACM William Sholto Douglas, Air Officer Commanding (AOC) Fighter Command, with a bar to the DFC for his successful leadership of No. 317 Squadron.

[302]: Similarly awarded, S/Ldr Jan Zumbach received his bar to the DFC from AVM Richard Ernest Saul, AOC No. 12 Group, on 6 October 1942 at RAF Kirton-in-Lindsey.

[303]: P/Os Mirosław Maciejowski (left) and Stanisław Brzeski were each decorated with the DFC by A/Cdre Wilfred Henry Dunn, AOC No. 81 Group, on 8 October 1942 at RAF Grangemouth.

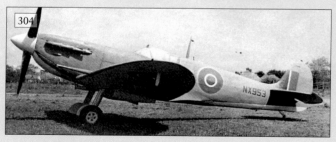

[304–305]: The Dieppe landings combined the efforts of the air force and the navy. The story of F/O Longin Majewski's Spitfire VB EN912 RF-M did so, too. It was seriously damaged during 'Jubilee': its shot up flaps failed during landing at Redhill, resulting in an overshoot. The aeroplane was sent away for repairs and eventually converted to Seafire IB standard for the Royal Navy, with a new serial number, NX953. It was then written off during the landing of Sub-Lt. R. D. Wood, No. 809 Sqn FAA, aboard HMS 'Unicorn' on 31 July 1943.

Appendix I – Summary of Operation 'Jubilee' in the Combat Diary of RAF Northolt

AUGUST 19th, 1942.

OPERATION   "JUBILEE".

GENERAL STORY

The general outline of the operation was to land Commando forces at beaches on the flanks of Dieppe, one about 3 miles E. but two landings to silence Coastal gun battery, one about 1 mile E. to silence a further gun battery, one about 1 mile W. to attack and destroy an enemy R.D.F. Station, and landings at two other beaches about 3 miles W. of Le Havre to seize and destroy Coastal gun battery.

These landings were to be followed by a frontal assault on the beach in front of the Dieppe Esplanade and the forces landed here were to endeavour to destroy various installations in Dieppe.

It was intended to penetrate as far as Dieppe/St. Aubin aerodrome and destroy installations there, and to attack a German Infantry Headquarters at Arques about 5 miles inland.

The result from the Army point of view was that the far west landing was completely successful and had left the Coast within three hours. The near west landing was successful in that it destroyed the R.D.F. Station and got some tanks through into Dieppe town. The near east landing was unfortunate in running into an enemy convoy on the approach to the beach, and was badly cut up - reformed later in the Operation and made a partially successful landing. The far east landing was badly beaten up and made no progress. The frontal assault never got through the wire, a number of tanks were abandoned on the beach and heavy casualties incurred.

The ground side of the air picture was that two areas, one being the race-course, were to be made available for crash landings if necessary. Only the race-course was made available and there were two instances of crash landings made, aircraft destroyed and pilots returning with the convoy.

From the Air/Sea Rescue point of view, most of the Air/Sea Rescue was mixed in with the Naval convoy (217 vessels including 6 destroyers in all). Two of the destroyers were equipped to act as Forward R/T Control Points.

From an air control point of view, there were many cases of cannon fighters taking off and going over from the Forward Control off the beach, and there being detailed to targets.

OPERATIONS BY THE COMMAND

The share of the Command in the combined operation against Dieppe began at approx. 0420 hours, when Bostons left to bomb and machine-gun gun emplacements. They were followed shortly afterwards by Hurricane/bombers, Hurricanes and Spitfires which attacked similar objectives, while fighters also provided escort for smoke-laying aircraft and covered the landing of our ground forces. This cover was continued while our troops consolidated their positions, and as a result of increased opposition as well as to cover/re-embarkation (timed to begin at 1050 hours) its volume was increased from 0730 hours onwards.

At 1005 hours, four Squadrons of Spitfires IX with 24 Fortresses of the U.S.A. 8th Army Air Force Bomber Command which bombed Abbeville/Drucat aerodrome from 23,000 ft. at approximately 1035 hours. The bombing was extremely accurate. Photographic evidence shows that hits were scored on dispersal areas, runways and flak opposition. There are indications that enemy aircraft were diverted from the aerodrome about half an hour after the attack, but that it was serviceable again by the evening. It is considered, however, that a number of aircraft are likely to have been destroyed or damaged on the ground and that considerable damage must have been done to facilities. All the Fortresses returned safely. As a result of combats, one F.W. 190 was damaged for the loss of one Spitfire, the pilot of which was wounded but is safe.

Cover was continued during the re-embarkation of our ground forces, escort was again given to smoke-laying aircraft, and enemy positions were attacked by fighters and escorted Bomber Command Bostons. During this phase of the operation, a wing of Typhoons carried out a diversion in the Ostend area. In the afternoon and evening further cover (including the laying of additional smoke screens) was given to our forces as they withdrew across the Channel.

In addition to these offensive operations, a number of defensive patrols were flown to intercept enemy aircraft operating against our shipping and coastal objectives in southern England. Mustangs of Army Co-operation Command carried out tactical reconnaissance sorties throughout the operation.

ENEMY ACTIVITY

Although enemy aircraft were sighted in small numbers almost from the start of the operation, air opposition does not appear to have developed intensively until about four hours after dawn. Thereafter the enemy used his a/c as follows:-

Fighters and fighter/bombers

Single-engined fighters operated intensively throughout the day. The nature of the operation makes it very difficult to estimate the scale of effort, but a consideration of the available evidence suggest that the enemy probably carried out about 700 fighters and fighter/bomber sorties over the area of the operation and against our shipping off the French Coast. This effort was devoted mainly to attacking our aircraft and providing escort, and more particularly cover for bombers. Fighter/bombers, which do not appear to have operated on a major scale, attacked our aircraft and are reported to have been seen in formations of up to 15 aircraft. Fighter activity appears to have been particularly intense from 0630 to 1015 hours, from 1200 to 1300 hours and from 1415 to 1500 hours. In addition to this defensive activity, two F.W.190's flew over Shoreham early in the morning, and in the afternoon two Me.109's dropped bombs at Selsey and six F.W.190's bombed and machine-gunned trawlers off the Sussex Coast.

Long Range Bombers

It is estimated that the enemy made a total of 125 long-range bomber sorties. Some 75 of them were carried out over the area of operations and against our shipping off the French Coast. In addition, some 15 long-range bombers carried out shipping reconnaissance off the East and South coasts. A trawler was attacked off Cromer at 1500 hours. Between 1545 and 1930 hours a total of about 37 a/c operated over the Portsmouth/Southampton area, dropping bombs with little effect in Hampshire, West Sussex and the Isle of Wight. Four H.E. fell on an aerodrome, causing slight damage.

By 1000 hours, i.e. five hours after landing, the enemy brought in night bomber forces from Holland and Belgium and Central France, and two Squadrons of Training Bombers.

Bomber Reconnaissances

Normal reconnaissances were carried out, including routine weather flights. In addition to the shipping reconnaissances carried out by long-range bombers, reconnaissance aircraft made about the usual number of sorties off the East Coast and approximately three times as many over the Channel. In the morning an a/c on reconnaissance flew over Southwold and another over Northern Ireland. Four a/c flew over the Portsmouth/Southampton area, possibly on a visual reconnaissance, between two phases of the attack referred to in paragraph above.

TYPES OF AIRCRAFT OPERATING UNDER THE CONTROL OF 11 GROUP

Fighter Command		
	Hurricane 1, 11.	6 Sqdns. Close Support.
	Hurricane/bombers	2 Squadrons.
(55 squadrons.	Spitfire V,1X.	50 Squadrons Cover.
(3 U.S.A. Sqdns.	Typhoons	
	Bostons - Intruders	
	Beaufighters.	
Army Co-operation Command		
	Blenheims	3 Squadrons
	Mustangs	4 Squadrons.
Bomber Command		
	Bostons - 2 Group	2 Squadrons.

Summary of Operation 'Jubilee' and its air force aspects in the RAF Northolt Combat Diary. The crucial statistics for assessment of the Polish contribution were are follows:

- *62 Allied squadrons of single-engined fighters, including 50 for air cover (Spitfires and Typhoons), 8 for direct ground support (Hurricanes) and 4 for reconnaissance (Mustang);*
- *58 Allied fighter pilots killed or missing;*
- *88 Allied fighter aircraft destroyed or missing;*
- *90 ½ enemy aircraft destroyed, 43 probably destroyed and 151 damaged credited by Fighter Command to the pilots.*

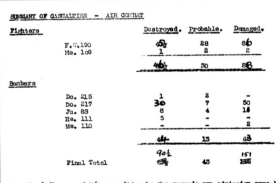

SUMMARY OF CASUALTIES - AIR COMBAT

Fighters		Destroyed.	Probable.	Damaged.
	F.W.190	45½	28	86
	Me.109	1	2	2
		46½	30	88
Bombers				
	Do.215	1	2	-
	Do.217	30	7	50
	Ju.88	8	4	11
	He.111	5	-	-
	Me.110	-	-	2
		44	13	63
Final Total		90½	43	151

The final figures of E/A casualties by the enemy's own admission were between 150 and 200 aircraft.

OUR CASUALTIES

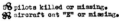

58 pilots killed or missing.
88 aircraft cat "E" or missing.

3 Bostons of Bomber Command & crews missing.

9 Mustang pilots and 1 Blenheim of Army Co-op. Command missing.

Polish Wings

NORTHOLT POLISH WING

Operation "Jubilee" August 19th, 1942.

303 Squadron operated from Redhill
302 and 308 Squadrons operated from Heston
306 and 317 Squadrons operated from Northolt.

The Wing flew eight sorties during the day, each of 302, 303, 306, 308, 317 (Polish) squadrons flew four sorties.

The stories of 302, 306 and 308 Squadrons are those of work well done, but no conclusive combat with the enemy. Bombers were escorted, and other squadrons of the Wing - whilst in combat - were protected from attack, for the loss of one pilot of 308 squadron.

303 and 317 Squadrons were so fortunate as to be able to carry the attack to the enemy, and on three of the Wing sorties were able to destroy 13½, probably destroy 5 and damage 3 others for the loss of one pilot only, from 303 Squadron.

1) 0500-0715
50 Spitfires VB, 302, 308, 306, 317 Squadrons, S/L Nowierski and G/C Paulikowski. The Wing patrolled off Dieppe between 6/11,000 ft. and encountered a few small formations of F.W. 190's and Me.109's. In a sharp attack on 317 Squadron, F/O Cholewka was wounded who, with his right arm useless owing to enemy cannon strike, hovering between consciousness and unconsciousness through loss of blood, returned from France and putting down his undercarriage with his left hand, holding the stick between his knees, locked the undercarriage with his foot and made a perfect landing at Lympne. He taxied the aircraft to the perimeter, switched off his engine, and waited to be lifted out and taken to hospital.

Enemy casualties:- Nil
Our Casualties :- 1 Spitfire VB (308) Cat E. not due to enemy action.
F/O Cholewka (317) wounded.

2) 0930-1145
26 Spitfires, 303, 317, W/C Janus and S/Ldr. Nowierski patrolled in target area at 8,000 ft. and were engaged all the time with many enemy fighters and bombers. W/C Janus & S/Ldr. Nowierski. With the squadrons actively engaged with enemy bombers fighters, the W/C Flying and his No. 2 dived on and split up a formation of bombers which were about to attack the shipping, causing the bombers to jettison their bombs and return towards land in disorder. S/Ldr. Nowierski damaged 2 Do.217's.

303 Sqdn. The Sqdn, seeing F.W.190's bombing the beaches and then joining the combat over the ships, went into the fight over the ships. Soon afterwards an R/T warning of bombers was received and the Squadron Commander split off his outside sections to attack the bombers whilst the rest remained to engage the fighters.

317 Sqdn. The Squadron was below the bombers when the R/T warning from the W/C was received and started to climb to them - seeing the bombers split up by the attack of the W/C and his No. 2 the Squadron attacked 3 F.W.190's at the same height and then patrolling in loose fours over the ships engaged various a/c in combat. F/O Maciejowski reported that the port engine of a Ju.88 he attacked blew up and fell out, taking the mainplane with it. Throughout the battle, Sqdns. of the Wing provided an umbrella for the battle below.

Enemy casualties:-
1 F.W.190 destroyed.	S/Ldr. Zumbach	303	
1 F.W.190 probable		303	
1 Ju.88 destroyed	F/O Socha	303	
1 F.W.190 destroyed		303	
1 Ju.88 destroyed	F/O Kolecki	303	
1 F.W.190 probable	F/O Glowacki	303	
1 F.W.190 probable	F/Lt. Horciniak	303	
1 F.W.190 probable	Sgt. Karczmarz	303	
1 F.W.190 probable	F/Sgt. Giermer	303	
1 Do.217 destroyed	F/Lt. Rutkowski	317	
1 Ju.88 destroyed	F/O Maciejowski	317	
1 F.W.190 destroyed		317	
1 F.W.190 damaged	Sgt. Paulowski	317	
2 Do.217 damaged	S/L Nowierski	Wing	

3) 1020-1205
24 Spitfires VB. 302 and 308 Squadrons were despatched to escort 6 Bostons. From rendezvous at Selsey Bill at 1040, they proceeded to target area, flying at 2,500 ft. Many a/c were seen, no engagement took place. Bombs were not seen to fall and the ships were laying smoke screens.

4) 1055-1250
12 Spitfires VB, 306 Sqdn. escorted 6 smoke-screen laying Blenheims from Selsey Bill. No engagement took place, one pilot seen in his dinghy and reported, a fix being given.

5) 1330-1425
12 Spitfires VB, 306 Sqdn. were despatched to escort 5 Blenheims which were to lay a smoke screen. Operation was cancelled and the squadron recalled.

6) 1245-1425
47 Spitfires VB, 302, 303, 308, 317 Sqdns and S/L Nowierski were detailed to patrol target area at 5,000 ft. with two Biggin Hill squadrons. The other Sqdns. were not seen. F.W.'s were found at 5,000 ft. about 20 in number, trying to dive-bomb the shipping. These aircraft were immediately engaged by 303 Sqdn. In each of the successful combats, the enemy pilot was seen to bale out over the convoy which by this time had split up and spread out to about 10 miles off Dieppe. One large ship with stern towards land, was motionless, and was soon to explode throwing smoke up to 5,000 ft.

Enemy casualties:-
1 F.W.190 destroyed.	F/O Horbaczewski	303
1 F.W.190 destroyed	Sgt. Stasik	303
1 F.W.190 destroyed	F/Sgt. Popek	303

7) 1535-1725
52 Spitfires VB, 302, 303, 306, 308, 317 Sqdns, W/C Janus, S/L Nowierski, W/C Rolski, S/L Kolaczkowski were despatched to patrol over the convoy. 302 and 308 patrolled above cloud, and the remainder below cloud. Various a/c more encountered attempting to attack the shipping. The weather was deteriorating rapidly and at the time of this patrol was 7/10 cloud at 2,500/10,000 ft. with two layers of 10/10 base above.

303 Sqdn. Arriving with the rest of the Wing over the convoy when it was at about mid-Channel on its return, the Sqdn. saw 2 He.111 about to carry out a bombing attack - the Sqdn. immediately attacked and caused the E/A to jettison their bombs and make for home. They were chased and shot down - several pilots sharing the destruction. The pilots had to wait their turn to get in an attack, and one pilot reported being pushed out of the fight by another pilot who was anxious to conclude matters. Sgt. Mokitniski's Spitfire was repeatedly holed by cannon shells from 3 F.W.190's but he brought his a/c back to base, himself untouched.

317 Sqdn. Joining in the attack started by 303 Sqdn, further enemy bombers and fighters were encountered and under the fighter umbrella provided by other Sqdns. of the Wing, successful engagements took place.

Enemy casualties:-
1 He.111 destroyed.	F/O Glowacki	303
	Sgt. Butecki	303
	Sgt. Mokitniski	303
1 He.111 destroyed	F/Lt. Rutkowski	317
	F/O Brzeski	317
1 F.W.190 destroyed	F/O Lukaszewicz	317
1 Do.217 destroyed	F/O Maciejowski	317
	Sgt. Kolesynski	317
1 He.111 destroyed	F/O Anbach	303
	F/Sgt. Giermer	303
	F/Sgt. Gatranko	317

Our casualties:-
P/O Dann 303 + }
F/O Landsman 306 } Missing
2 Spitfires VB

+ INFORMED 24/9/42 - P/W.

8) 1830-1945
12 Spitfires VB 303 Sqdn. were despatched to patrol convoy South of Selsey Bill. The convoy was soon to be splitting up and the weather was getting bad, 10/10 cloud with Base at 4,000 ft.

SUMMARY OF CASUALTIES

Enemy			Destroyed.	Probable.	Damaged.
	303 Sqdn.	F.W.190	4	5	-
		Ju.88	2		-
		He.111	1½/3rds		
			8.1/8th	5	
	317 Sqdn.	F.W.190	2	-	1
		Ju.88	1	-	-
		He.111	2.1/3	-	-
		Do.217	2		
			7.1/3		1
	S/Ldr. Nowierski	Do.217			2

TOTAL. 15½ destroyed, 5 probable, 3 damaged.

Our casualties
F/O Dann	303	Missing P/W.
F/O Landsman	306	Missing
F/O Cholewka	317	Wounded

1 Spitfire VB, 303, Missing
1 Spitfire VB, 303, Cat B.
1 Spitfire VB, 306, Missing.

NOTE
The reasons for the small losses suffered by the Wing are considered to be as follows:-
1) On the way out, the Wing economised on patrol (1800 revs. and 0 boost) and during the patrol a high constant speed was maintained (2850/2600 revs. plus two boost to plus 4 boost) thus giving pilots every chance to take avoiding action and to make contacts.
2) The sections in each Sqdn. remained in close contact and were always effectively covering each other.
3) Height was always maintained, and if a pilot dived down to attack, he returned to the formation even when he had used all his ammunition. This was done because all pilots knew their allotted patrol area and were easily able to make rendezvous amongst themselves.
4) Withdrawal was made in good order on the order of the Wing/Commander when he was satisfied that the relieving Squadrons had effectively taken up their positions.

Summary of Operation 'Jubilee' actions by the 1st Polish Wing, as described in the RAF Northolt Combat Diary. The following statistics of the 1st Polish Wing effort is obtained from comparison of the two summaries:
- the wing contributed 10% of the air cover squadrons and 8% of all single-engined fighter squadrons;
- the wing lost 3.5% of all Allied fighter pilots killed or missing;
- the wing lost 3.4% of all Allied fighter aircraft destroyed or missing;
- the wing was credited by Fighter Command with 17% of all enemy aircraft destroyed.

Appendix II – Operational missions flown by Polish units during Operation 'Jubilee'

Pilot			Aircraft		Notes
Northolt Wing HQ					
S/Ldr	Tadeusz	Nowierski	BL412	ZF-C[1]	
G/Cpt	Stefan	Pawlikowski	EN916	JH-J	guest, HQ Fighter Command officer
No. 306 Sqn (Northolt)					
S/Ldr	Tadeusz	Czerwiński	EN826	UZ-C	
F/Lt	Wieńczysław	Barański	AR337	UZ-A	guest, No. 308 Sqn Ops Room controller
F/O	Władysław	Walendowski	W3774?	UZ-K	
F/O	Eugeniusz	Krzemiński	BM537	UZ-G	
F/O	Stanisław	Kędzierski	AR428	UZ-J	
P/O	Władysław	Potocki	R6904	UZ-D	
P/O	Józef	Jeka	(?)	UZ-T	
P/O	Jerzy	Polak	AA930	UZ-P	
F/O	Emil	Landsman	BM424	UZ-S	
F/Sgt	Wawrzyniec	Jasiński	R6770	UZ-V	
F/Sgt	Marcin	Machowiak	BL240	UZ-U	
Sgt	Stefan	Czachla	AD581	UZ-M	pilot slightly injured, Spitfire destroyed
No. 317 Sqn (Northolt)					
S/Ldr	Stanisław	Skalski	BM131	JH-Q	
F/Lt	Kazimierz	Rutkowski	BL690	JH-Z	
F/O	Jerzy	Mencel	AB925	JH-F	
F/O	Marian	Cholewka	AR340	JH-P	pilot seriously wounded, Spitfire damaged
F/O	Zbigniew	Janicki	BL481	JH-Y	
F/O	Witold	Łanowski	BM566	JH-S	
F/O	Florian	Martini	BL860	JH-T	
F/O	Przesław	Sadowski	EN896	JH-X	
P/O	Stanisław	Łukaszewicz	AR424	JH-A	
P/O	Tadeusz	Felc	BL927	JH-L	
F/Sgt	Kazimierz	Sztramko	AD269	JH-B	
Sgt	Władysław	Grobelny	BM481	JH-H	
No. 302 Sqn (Heston)					
F/Lt	Stanisław	Łapka	EN865	WX-L	
F/Lt	Marian	Chełmecki	EN861	WX-N	
F/O	Tadeusz	Ciastuła	AA856	WX-H[2]	
F/O	Zbigniew	Wróblewski	BM651	WX-D	
F/O	Tadeusz	Kwiatkowski	BM648	WX-R	
P/O	Jerzy	Urbański	BM179	WX-A	
P/O	Tadeusz	Zdzitowiecki	EN852	WX-M	
P/O	Marian	Wędzik	BL235	WX-W	
F/Sgt	Kazimierz	Kobusiński	AD317	WX-K	
Sgt	Eustachy	Łucyszyn	AR385	WX-J	
Sgt	Adam	Tiahnybok	EN922	WX-U	
Sgt	Władysław	Gretkierewicz	W3960	WX-O	

1   S/Ldr Nowierski flew Spitfire AD451 JH-N to Heston the day before and returned in it to Northolt following this operation, but used a No. 308 Sqn aeroplane to lead this mission from Heston. This may have been due to some petty technical problem with AD451, which then flew two sorties in the afternoon, in the hands of two pilots of No. 317 Sqn (F/Lt Rutkowski used it to claim an He 111 destroyed).

2   Recent research has revealed that AA856 was transferred from 'B' to 'A' Flight in August 1942 and the code was changed from WX-Z to WX-H. It was coded WX-H when lost on 8 September 1942 with P/O Jerzy Urbański (not WX-Z as stated erroneously in PW30).

Pilot			Aircraft		Notes
No. 308 Sqn (Heston)					
S/Ldr	Walerian	Żak	BL239	ZF-Q	
F/Lt	Jerzy	Popławski	EP171	ZF-Z?	
F/O	Brunon	Kudrewicz	BL436	ZF-E?	
F/O	Olgierd	Iliński	BL613	ZF-(?)	
F/O	Bolesław	Palej	BM538	ZF-R	
P/O	Tadeusz	Schiele	AD177	ZF-(?)	
P/O	Donat	Mickiewicz	W3313	ZF-(?)	
P/O	Bronisław	Mach	EN800	ZF-P?	
F/Sgt	Władysław	Majchrzyk	AB273	ZF-Y?	
F/Sgt	Stefan	Krzyżagórski	AA967	ZF-(?)	
Sgt	Feliks	Marek	W3510	ZF-(?)	
Sgt	Wacław	Korwel	BL545	ZF-(?)	
	5:30-5:50	**ASR patrol (cancelled)**			
No. 302 Sqn (Heston)					
F/O	Eugeniusz	Ebenrytter	W3902	WX-T	
P/O	Andrzej	Beyer	AA853	WX-C	
Sgt	Hipolit	Mikusek	AA854	WX-G	
	9:30-11:30	**Patrol over Dieppe**			
Northolt Wing HQ					
W/Cdr	Stefan	Janus	EN916	JH-J	
S/Ldr	Tadeusz	Nowierski	BL860	JH-T	0–0–2 Do 217
No. 317 Sqn (Northolt)					
S/Ldr	Stanisław	Skalski	BM131	JH-Q	
F/Lt	Kazimierz	Rutkowski	BL690	JH-Z	1–0–0 Do 217
F/O	Roman	Hrycak	BL410	JH-D	
F/O	Zbigniew	Janicki	BL481	JH-Y	
P/O	Stanisław	Łukaszewicz	AR424	JH-A	
P/O	Michał	Maciejowski	BL927	JH-L[3]	1–0–0 FW 190 & 1–0–0 Ju 88
F/Sgt	Kazimierz	Sztramko	AD295	JH-C	
F/Sgt	Ryszard	Lewczyński	BM566	JH-S	
Sgt	Wacław	Frączek	AB925	JH-F	
Sgt	Adam	Kolczyński	AD269	JH-B	
Sgt	Władysław	Pawłowski	AA758	JH-V	0–0–1 FW 190; Spitfire damaged
Sgt	Werner	Kirchner	EN896	JH-X	
No. 303 Sqn (Redhill)					
S/Ldr	Jan	Zumbach	EP594	RF-D	1–1–0 FW 190
F/Lt	Janusz	Marciniak	W3893	RF-U	0–1–0 FW 190
P/O	Czesław	Mroczyk	AR318	RF-L	
P/O	Tadeusz	Kołecki	AB183	RF-A	1–0–0 Ju 88
P/O	Stanisław	Socha	BL670	RF-K	1–0–0 Ju 88 & 1–0–0 FW 190
P/O	Antoni	Głowacki	AB174	RF-Q	0–1–0 FW 190
F/Sgt	Kazimierz	Wünsche	AR371	RF-B	
F/Sgt	Wacław	Giermer	BM540	RF-I	0–1–0 FW 190
F/Sgt	Jan	Palak	AA913	RF-P	
Sgt	Józef	Karczmarz	BL567	RF-T	0–1–0 FW 190; Spitfire damaged
Sgt	Włodzimierz	Chojnacki	BL748	RF-W	
Sgt	Stanisław	Górny	AA839	RF-S	
	10:20-12:00	**Escort to smoke-laying Bostons**			

3   'AD295' is listed in the ORB as the Spitfire he flew (and quoted in numerous publications, including my PW29), but the document listed the same serial for F/Sgt Sztramko during the mission. Sztramko's flying log book confirms he flew AD295 on that occasion. As most pilots flew the same aircraft during the 9.30 and 15.50 missions, it can be guessed that P/O Maciejowski used BL927 during that sortie. Note that the ORB of No. 317 Sqn for 1942 has an enormous number of incorrect aircraft serial number entries, so quite many serials in this table differ from those in the ORB.

Pilot		Aircraft		Notes
No. 302 Sqn (Heston)				
F/Lt	Stanisław	Łapka	EN865	WX-L	
F/O	Alojzy	Rodziewicz	BM651	WX-D	
F/O	Józef	Regulski	W3960	WX-O	
F/O	Kazimierz	Sporny	EN922	WX-U	
F/O	Eugeniusz	Ebenrytter	EN852	WX-M	
P/O	Andrzej	Beyer	AR385	WX-J	
P/O	Marian	Rytka	BM648	WX-R	
P/O	Czesław	Śnieć	BL925	WX-Y	
Sgt	Ignacy	Czajka	AA856	WX-H	
Sgt	Hipolit	Mikusek	AA854	WX-G	
Sgt	Kazimierz	Benziński	W3954	WX-B	
Sgt	Erwin	Janusz	EN861	WX-N	
No. 308 Sqn (Heston)				
S/Ldr	Walerian	Żak	BL239	ZF-Q	
F/Lt	Jerzy	Popławski	EP171	ZF-Z?	
F/Lt	Tadeusz	Koc	BL977	ZF-A?	
F/O	Zbigniew	Kobierzycki	BL545	ZF-(?)	
F/O	Jan	Jakubowski	W3313	ZF-(?)	
F/O	Jan	Błaszczyk	P8561	ZF-B?	
P/O	Tadeusz	Stabrowski	AB273	ZF-Y?	
P/O	Marian	Kotlarz	W3630	ZF-(?)	
P/O	Stanisław	Madej	W3510	ZF-(?)	
F/Sgt	Jan	Okrój	AD177	ZF-(?)	
Sgt	Jan	Osoba	AA967	ZF-(?)	
Sgt	Władysław	Sznapka	AB275	ZF-M	
10:55-12:50	**Escort to smoke-laying Blenheims**			
No. 306 Sqn (Northolt)				
F/Lt	Józef	Gil	W3774?	UZ-K	
F/Lt	Józef	Żulikowski	AR327	UZ-Z[4]	
F/O	Bohdan	Arct	AR337	UZ-A	Spitfire damaged
F/O	Witold	Szyszkowski	AR336	UZ-O	
F/O	Stanisław	Marcisz	BL240	UZ-U	
F/O	Jan	Kurowski	AA930	UZ-P	
F/O	Sergiusz	Szpakowicz	AR381	UZ-R	
P/O	Henryk	Pietrzak	BM537	UZ-G	
P/O	Zygmunt	Jeliński	AR428	UZ-J	
P/O	Grzegorz	Sołogub	BM424	UZ-S	
F/Sgt	Zdzisław	Horn	R6770	UZ-V	
F/Sgt	Witold	Krupa	R6904	UZ-D	
12:45-14:35	**Cover to troop withdrawal from Dieppe**			
Northolt Wing HQ				
S/Ldr	Tadeusz	Nowierski	AD295	JH-C	
W/Cdr	Tadeusz	Rolski	BL860	JH-T	guest, HQ Fighter Command officer
No. 302 Sqn (Heston)				
F/Lt	Marian	Chełmecki	EN861	WX-N	
F/O	Tadeusz	Ciastuła	AA856	WX-H	
F/O	Zbigniew	Wróblewski	BM651	WX-D	
P/O	Tadeusz	Zdzitowiecki	EN852	WX-M	
P/O	Marian	Wędzik	BL235	WX-W	
P/O	Jerzy	Urbański	AA853	WX-C	

4   It is likely that this Spitfire was coded UZ-Ż for Żulikowski, as was his subsequent Spitfire IX BS456, and later his Mustang III KH507.

Pilot			Aircraft		Notes
F/Sgt	Kazimierz	Kobusiński	AD317	WX-K	
Sgt	Władysław	Gretkierewicz	W3960	WX-O	
Sgt	Adam	Tiahnybok	EN922	WX-U	
Sgt	Eustachy	Łucyszyn	AR385	WX-J	
No. 308 Sqn (Heston)					
S/Ldr	Walerian	Żak	BL239	ZF-Q	
F/Lt	Jerzy	Popławski	EP171	ZF-Z?	
F/O	Józef	Sobolewski	AA967	ZF-(?)	
F/O	Bolesław	Palej	BM538	ZF-R	
F/O	Brunon	Kudrewicz	BL436	ZF-E?	
F/O	Jan	Błaszczyk	P8561	ZF-B?	
P/O	Bronisław	Mach	EN800	ZF-P?	
P/O	Stanisław	Madej	BL412	ZF-C	
P/O	Donat	Mickiewicz	W3313	ZF-(?)	
P/O	Tadeusz	Schiele	AD177	ZF-(?)	
F/Sgt	Władysław	Majchrzyk	AB273	ZF-Y?	
Sgt	Wacław	Korwel	AB275	ZF-M	
No. 317 Sqn (Northolt)					
F/Lt	Marian	Trzebiński	AR424	JH-A	
F/O	Jerzy	Mencel	AB925	JH-F	
F/O	Teofil	Szymankiewicz	BL927	JH-L	
F/O	Witold	Łanowski	BL481	JH-Y	
F/O	Przesław	Sadowski	EN896	JH-X	
F/O	Stanisław	Bochniak	BM131	JH-Q	
F/O	Florian	Martini	AD451	JH-N	
P/O	Jerzy	Zbrożek	BL410	JH-D	
P/O	Tadeusz	Felc	AD269	JH-B	
F/Sgt	Tadeusz	Hanzelka	BM566	JH-S	
Sgt	Władysław	Grobelny	BM481	JH-H	
No. 303 Sqn (Redhill)					
F/Lt	Zygmunt	Bieńkowski	BM144	RF-H	
F/O	Eugeniusz	Horbaczewski	AR366[5]	RF-C	1–0–0 FW 190
F/O	Longin	Majewski	EN912	RF-M	Spitfire damaged
F/O	Antoni	Kolubiński	AR376	RF-R	
P/O	Mirosław	Szelestowski	BM531	RF-V	
P/O	Stefan	Baran	AA839	RF-S	
P/O	Zbigniew	Wojda	AA913	RF-P	
F/Sgt	Mieczysław	Popek	BL670	RF-K	½–0–0 FW 190
F/Sgt	Mieczysław	Adamek	BL748	RF-W	
Sgt	Ryszard	Górecki	BM540	RF-I	
Sgt	Arkadiusz	Bondarczuk	BL594[5]	RF-G	
Sgt	Józef	Stasik	BL574	RF-F	1–0–0 FW 190
13:45-14:25	**Escort to smoke-laying Blenheims (cancelled)**				
No. 306 Sqn (Northolt)					
S/Ldr	Tadeusz	Czerwiński	EN826	UZ-C	
F/O	Władysław	Walendowski	W3774?	UZ-K	
F/O	Eugeniusz	Krzemiński	BM537	UZ-G	
F/O	Stanisław	Kędzierski	AR428	UZ-J	
F/O	Ryszard	Malczewski	AR381	UZ-R	
F/O	Emil	Landsman	BM424	UZ-S	
P/O	Władysław	Potocki	R6904	UZ-D	

5 Serial numbers as listed in the ORB, but one Polish document mentions Horbaczewski's aircraft during that mission as 'G' and Bondarczuk's as 'C'. Notably, BL594 RF-G was Horbaczewski's usual mount, so it is not impossible that their ORB entries were mistaken.

Pilot			Aircraft		Notes
P/O	Józef	Jeka	(?)	UZ-T	
F/Sgt	Wawrzyniec	Jasiński	R6770	UZ-V	
F/Sgt	Marcin	Machowiak	BL240	UZ-U	
Sgt	Jan A.	Rogowski	AB192	UZ-L	
Sgt	Marian	Kordasiewicz	AR336	UZ-O	
	15:50-17:20	Convoy patrol off Dieppe			
	Northolt Wing HQ				
W/Cdr	Stefan	Janus	EN916	JH-J	
S/Ldr	Tadeusz	Nowierski	BM481	JH-H	
W/Cdr	Tadeusz	Rolski	BL860	JH-T	guest, HQ Fighter Command officer
S/Ldr	Wojciech	Kołaczkowski	EN896	JH-X	guest, HQ Fighter Command officer
	No. 306 Sqn (Northolt)				
S/Ldr	Tadeusz	Czerwiński	EN826	UZ-C	
F/O	Władysław	Walendowski	W3774?	UZ-K	
F/O	Eugeniusz	Krzemiński	BM537	UZ-G	
F/O	Stanisław	Kędzierski	AR428	UZ-J	
F/O	Ryszard	Malczewski	AR381	UZ-R	
F/O	Emil	Landsman	BM424	UZ-S	pilot in captivity, Spitfire lost in sea
P/O	Władysław	Potocki	R6904	UZ-D	
P/O	Józef	Jeka	(?)	UZ-T	
F/Sgt	Wawrzyniec	Jasiński	R6770	UZ-V	
F/Sgt	Marcin	Machowiak	BL240	UZ-U	
Sgt	Jan A.	Rogowski	AB192	UZ-L	
Sgt	Marian	Kordasiewicz	AR336	UZ-O	
	No. 317 Sqn (Northolt)				
S/Ldr	Stanisław	Skalski	BM131	JH-Q	
F/Lt	Kazimierz	Rutkowski	AD451	JH-N	1–0–0 He 111
F/O	Roman	Hrycak	BL410	JH-D	
P/O	Stanisław	Łukaszewicz	AR424	JH-A	1–0–0 FW 190
P/O	Michał	Maciejowski	BL927	JH-L	½–0–0 Do 217; Spitfire damaged
P/O	Stanisław	Brzeski	BM566	JH-S	1–0–0 He 111
F/Sgt	Kazimierz	Sztramko	AD295	JH-C	⅓–0–0 He 111
Sgt	Wacław	Frączek	AB925	JH-F	
Sgt	Adam	Kolczyński	AD269	JH-B	½–0–0 Do 217
Sgt	Werner	Kirchner	BL481	JH-Y	
	No. 302 Sqn (Heston)				
S/Ldr	Julian	Kowalski	EN865	WX-L	
F/O	Alojzy	Rodziewicz	BM651	WX-D	
F/O	Kazimierz	Sporny	EN922	WX-U	
F/O	Eugeniusz	Ebenrytter	BM648	WX-R	
F/O	Józef	Regulski	W3960	WX-O	
P/O	Andrzej	Beyer	AR385	WX-J	
P/O	Marian	Rytka	EN852	WX-M	
P/O	Czesław	Śnieć	BL925	WX-Y	
Sgt	Ignacy	Czajka	BM179	WX-A	
Sgt	Kazimierz	Benziński	W3954	WX-B	
Sgt	Hipolit	Mikusek	AD317	WX-K	
Sgt	Erwin	Janusz	EN861	WX-N	
	No. 308 Sqn (Heston)				
F/Lt	Tadeusz	Koc	BL977	ZF-A?	
F/O	Jan	Jakubowski	W3313	ZF-(?)	
F/O	Olgierd	Iliński	AD177	ZF-(?)	
F/O	Bolesław	Palej	BM538	ZF-R	

Polish Wings

Pilot			Aircraft		Notes
F/O	Zbigniew	Kobierzycki	BL545	ZF-(?)	
P/O	Marian	Kotlarz	W3630	ZF-(?)	
P/O	Tadeusz	Stabrowski	AB273	ZF-Y?	
F/Sgt	Władysław	Majchrzyk	BL940	ZF-V	
F/Sgt	Stefan	Krzyżagórski	AA967	ZF-(?)	
Sgt	Stanisław	Domański	P8561	ZF-B?	
Sgt	Tadeusz	Turek	BL412	ZF-C	
Sgt	Władysław	Sznapka	AB275	ZF-M	
		No. 303 Sqn (Redhill)			
S/Ldr	Jan	Zumbach	EP594	RF-D	⅓–0–0 He 111
F/Lt	Janusz	Marciniak	W3893	RF-U	
P/O	Tadeusz	Kołecki	AB183	RF-A	
P/O	Czesław	Mroczyk	AR318	RF-L	
P/O	Adam	Damm	BL574	RF-F	pilot killed, Spitfire lost in sea
P/O	Antoni	Głowacki	AB174	RF-Q	⅓–0–0 He 111
F/Sgt	Wacław	Giermer	BM540	RF-I	⅓–0–0 He 111
F/Sgt	Jan	Palak	AA913	RF-P	
Sgt	Aleksander	Rokitnicki	AR366	RF-C	⅓–0–0 He 111; Spitfire damaged
Sgt	Włodzimierz	Chojnacki	BL748	RF-W	
Sgt	Alojzy	Rutecki	BM531	RF-V	⅓–0–0 He 111
Sgt	Józef	Karczmarz	AA839	RF-S	
	16:25-17:30	Scramble over own base			
		No. 306 Sqn (Northolt)			
F/Lt	Józef	Gil	R6904?	UZ-D?[6]	
P/O	Grzegorz	Sołogub	AR428?	UZ-J?[6]	
	18:30-19:45	Convoy patrol between Beachy Head and Selsey Bill			
		No. 303 Sqn (Redhill)			
F/Lt	Zygmunt	Bieńkowski	BM144	RF-H	
F/O	Eugeniusz	Horbaczewski	BL594	RF-G	
F/O	Longin	Majewski	W3893	RF-U	
F/O	Antoni	Kolubiński	AR376	RF-R	
P/O	Zbigniew	Wojda	AA913	RF-P	
P/O	Mirosław	Szelestowski	BM531	RF-V	
P/O	Stefan	Baran	AA839	RF-S	
F/Sgt	Mieczysław	Popek	AR371	RF-B	
F/Sgt	Mieczysław	Adamek	BL748	RF-W	
Sgt	Ryszard	Górecki	BM540	RF-I	
Sgt	Arkadiusz	Bondarczuk	AR318	RF-L	
Sgt	Józef	Stasik	AB183	RF-A	

6   Code letters D and J were entered in No. 306 Sqn flight logs, but R6904 UZ-D and AR428 UZ-J were presumably still on convoy patrol at that time, flown by P/O Potocki and F/O Kędzierski, respectively.

Appendix III – Narrative sections of Polish pilots' personal combat reports for Operation 'Jubilee'

S/Ldr Tadeusz Nowierski, Wing HQ, 10.30

After reaching the patrol area I saw 5 Do. 217 approaching the convoy in vic-formation from the east at 8,000 ft. Above them I noticed a few F.W. 190. W/Comm. Janus and I immediately attacked the bombers from ahead to split up the formation and prevent them from reaching the convoy, and I fired 2 short cannon bursts at one of the e/a from 400 yards, which caused a small explosion in the port engine whereupon the e/a turned sharply to port and dived towards land. I followed it and fired three more bursts from cannon from 250 yards until my cannon ammunition was exhausted but saw no further results. The remaining four Do. 217 had broken formation and jettisoned their bombs about a mile away from the convoy. Shortly afterwards I noticed a Do. 217 diving towards the convoy and pull out at 3,000 ft., and fly towards Dieppe at high speed. I used emergency boost and caught up with the e/a at 1,000 ft over land south of Dieppe and fired several short bursts of m/g from 150-100 yards. I saw my bullets strike the fins and starboard main plane but could not stay to observe further results as I was being attacked by a F.W. 190. I therefore broke away and returning low to the patrol area noticed that there was complete quiet in the western part of Dieppe.

F/Lt Kazimierz Rutkowski, No. 317 Sqn, 10.30

When the Squadron was over the target and made a full turn to the left, I noticed several Do.217's in formation. When I was coming out of the sun with the squadron, I noticed a single Do.217 which was climbing towards the French coast, I left the formation and dived after him.
At a range of 500 yards I gave him two short cannon bursts, but did not notice results of same.
Then I caught up with him, and when at a range of 200 yards I gave him several short cannon bursts. I saw at first his airframe catch fire from the starboard engine and later parts of his plane dropping off. I fired my last burst at a range of less than 100 yards. Sgt.Pawlowski on my left saw the enemy a/c which I attacked catch fire.
I was warned then by Sgt.Pawlowski that Fw.190's were on our tail. Then they opened fire on us.
I made a sharp turn to the left and then saw the Do.217 crash and explode to the north of Dieppe.

[306]: A frame from the camera gun film of F/Lt Rutkowski.

306

P/O Michał Maciejowski, No. 317 Sqn, 10.30

When the Squadron was over the target and made a full turn to the left I noticed 6 Do.217's and 2 Fw.190's together with a Ju.88, who were bombing the ships. I could not see the results of the bombing.
After having released his bombs, the Ju.88 went in a dive towards France. I dived after him from 3,000 feet and gave him several short cannon bursts at a range of about 400 yards. After a short while, I saw his port engine explode. The port wing and the remains of the engine broke off the a/c.
I made a turn to the left, because I had noticed 3 a/c with queer markings. At first I thought they were Fw's, afterwards I recognised them as Spitfires with American markings. They joined me, and I was acting as their leader. The last I saw of the Ju.88, it was diving out of control towards the inland deeper than Dieppe.
With the Americans under my command, I returned to my original place of patrol, there I noticed 2 Fw.190's attacking a convoy. I attacked the one, who after having jettisoned his bombs was pulling out of the dive. I gave him a full burst from cannon and machine guns, and saw the pilot bale out. (xxxx)
at a range of 200 - 250. and saw the pilot bale out.

Sgt Władysław Pawłowski, No. 317 Sqn, 10.30

I was on the right of F/Lt.Rutkowski's No.2. and after making one orbit over the convoy I saw a Do.217 returning to France. I saw F/Lt.Rutkowski attack this Do.217 first and saw the starboard engine catch fire. I opened fire at long range and saw no result. I fired a second burst and noticed 3 Fw's about to attack F/Lt.Rutkowski, I warned him and I turned to engage them. I opened fire at one of the Fw's at 250-300 yds. with a long burst of cannon and machine guns, and I saw the wings and fuselage being hit, and afterwards I saw the Fw. side slip and dive towards the sea. I then gave several bursts at long range at another Fw. but did not see the result. I was pursued by Fw's but by manoeuvring succeeded in joining the Squadron over the convoy.

S/Ldr Jan Zumbach, No. 303 Sqn, 10.30

As we approached the French Coast I noticed several Do. 217 coming from the east at 8,000 feet, and a while later 3 J.U. 88. Seeing that the Do. 217 were being engaged by other Spitfires I ordered my port and starboard sections to attack the JU. 88's. At the same time I saw 2 F.W. 190's flying on my port side and fired two bursts at one of the e/a from 450 yds. After the second burst the e/a showed black smoke and dived steeply towards land and was probably destroyed. I turned and saw the J.U. 88 which was attacked by P/O Socha burst into flames. Immediately after that 2 F.W. 190 appeared about 500 ft. below on my port side and I attacked one from 100-150 yards giving 3 bursts. The e/a gave off some smoke and pieces broke off, and shortly afterwards it burst into flames and dived vertically.

F/Lt Janusz Marciniak, No. 303 Sqn, 10.30

When over the patrol area our squadron was turning left and I noticed two Fw.190's flying in the opposite direction at 6000 ft. As they were passing us, I made a sharp right turn to get on their tails and one of the e/a immediately dived on seeing me. The other continued to fly at the same height and I approached to 500 yards. The Fw. turned on its back and dived. I followed him in a dive and fired at him from 400 yards, when I was at about 1500 ft. The e/a went into a steeper dive and disappeared in the smoke from the ships at about 500 ft. I was immediately attacked by 2 Fw.190's out of sun, but escaped by a climb.

P/O Tadeusz Kołecki, No. 303 Sqn, 10.30

I was leading our port section off from over the convoy at about 2000 ft. and after a left turn spotted a FW. 190 which I attacked immediately from 150-200 yds. while the E/A was on its back, but saw no results as it dived away steeply. A little later when we were between the convoy and the French Coast I saw a JU. 88 approaching the convoy from land in a shallow dive. At the same moment my squadron leader ordered me to attack the JU 88 which I did and gave a long burst from 150-100 yds. I followed it down to 4/5000 ft. and after making sure no E/A was on my tail continued to follow the JU.88 to 3,000 ft. The hun went down and and when it touched the sea, exploded 300-500 yds. from the convoy.

P/O Stanisław Socha, No. 303 Sqn, 10.30

We were orbiting left over our ships at 9,000 feet when I noticed on my port side 2 F.W. 190's which were trying to escape towards France. Using full boost I got within 200 yards and gave two cannon bursts at one of the enemy aircraft resulting in pieces flying off the cockpit and flames and clouds of smoke enveloping the enemy air-craft. About three minutes later the Squadron Leader told us on the R/T that J. U. 88's were below to port. I half-rolled and dived at one J.U. 88 firing all armament from 250 - 300 yards. The J.U. 88 jettisoned its bombs into the sea, began to smoke heavily and S/L Zumbach saw it crash into the sea.

P/O Antoni Głowacki, No. 303 Sqn, 10.30

I was No.3 in the port section of 4 of my squadron, and when we reached the patrol area I noticed 1 Fw.190 to port. I attacked it from 30 degrees astern and from 400 yards fired one burst of 1½ seconds, cannon only. The e/a gave out blue smoke and dived vertically, I followed it down from 9,000 ft. and had to pull out at 1,000 ft. to avoid colliding with another aircraft, thus losing sight of the e/a, which was then about 200 ft. above the sea still diving vertically. Sgt.Gorny, our No.4, saw smoke suddenly appear from the Fw.190 which was still diving very close to the sea and disappeared in a cloud of smoke issuing from some of the ships. I claim this Fw.190 as destroyed. I climbed and seeing 2 more Fw.190's, I gave each a short burst from 400 - 500 yards, but saw no results and the e/a climbed into cloud.

F/Sgt Wacław Giermer, No. 303 Sqn, 10.30

I was flying as No. 4 in the leading section and when we approached the French Coast we were attacked by several FW. 190 at about 8000 ft. We turned sharply to port and got onto their tails, and I saw one of the E/A trailing dark smoke which I attacked with two sharp bursts from machine gun from 400 yds. astern. The FW. 190 rolled on its back and went down in a slow spin until it disappeared into cloud at about 3000 ft. F/Sgt. Winsche witnessed this combat.

Sgt Józef Karczmarz, No. 303 Sqn, 10.30

When at 9,500 ft. and turning over the convoy I noticed 1 Fw.190 below attacking 2 Spitfires. I attacked it with 2 bursts from 200 yds and it broke away by climbing and half-rolling then going down vertically. I followed him down at an indicated speed of 430mph. to 3000 ft. and the Fw. continued to dive vertically. I had to pull out to avoid crashing into the sea and I last saw the e/a still vertical at 600 ft. diving at about 450 mph or more. I looked for the e/a but could not find it again. This combat took place east of Dieppe, where I could not see any other aircraft, and I claim 1 Fw.190 probably destroyed.

F/O Eugeniusz Horbaczewski, No. 303 Sqn, 13.40

I was leading the port section of four of my Squadron near the convoy and saw two pairs of Fw.190's and went in to attack the pair ahead and slightly above. I was warned of e/a on my tail and had to break away, but immediately saw some Fw.190's dive bombing our ships. I turned towards these e/a, followed by my No.2 (Sgt.Stasik) and engaged them. I selected one F.W.190 and after my first burst it began to smoke and dive down. Following him, I fired again and saw the pilot bale out. Meanwhile Sgt.Stasik had attacked another Fw.190 which I saw burst into flames.

F/Sgt Mieczysław Popek, No. 303 Sqn, 13.40

After arriving over the patrol area, I saw about 20 Fw.190's in lose formation at various heights. I was flying at 6,000 ft. when I saw 1 Fw.190 being attacked by a Spitfire. At a range of 300 yds. I fired at the e/a from beam astern and saw it roll on its back and the pilot bale out. I do not know to which squadron the Spitfire belonged with which I shared the destruction of the Fw.190.

Sgt Józef Stasik, No. 303 Sqn, 13.40
(with a statement by F/Lt Zygmunt Bieńkowski)

I was flying in F/O Horbaczewski's section of four when I saw 2 Fw.190 in front and a little above. I gave a long burst with deflection at one of the e/a from 200 yds. and saw it dive towards the sea. A Spitfire then dived into my line of fire. I followed it and saw that it was unharmed. I next saw the parachute of the pilot who had bailed out from the e/a fired at by F/O Horbaczewski.

I saw that Sgt.Stasik was unable to follow his e/a down as some Spitfires were obstructing him, so I dived down following the e/a. Just as I was about to open fire, I saw the cockpit hood fly off in two pieces and the pilot bale out.

P/O Antoni Głowacki, No. 303 Sqn, 16.30

Leading the port section of four on a patrol over our ships, I noticed two He.111's approaching the convoy. The ships opened fire at the e/a and my squadron Commander ordered me to attack the lower He.111. Followed by two of my pilots, I chased the e/a and fired three long bursts from cannon and m/g, as a result of which the e/a issued black smoke from both engines and pieces began to break off. I broke away and Sgt.Rokitnicki and Sgt.Rutecki took up the attack, whereupon, I saw the He.111 crash into the sea.

Sgt Aleksander Rokitnicki, No. 303 Sqn, 16.30

Flying as No.4 in the port section of four, I followed two other of our aircraft to attack a He.111. I saw some light smoke coming from the e/a after a burst fired by our leader (P/O Glowacki) and after I had fired burst, the e/a crashed in the sea.
Then I spotted 4 Fw.190's and fired a long burst at one of them from a distance of about 250 yds, but had to break away immediately because of being attacked by other e/a. When turning I saw a Fw.190 spinning down and there were only three Fw.190's following me. After I had made a few turns the e/a gave up the pursuit.

Sgt Alojzy Rutecki, No. 303 Sqn, 16.30

Flying as No.2 in the port section of four, I attacked an He.111 with my leader P/O Glowacki. I fired the first burst (cannons and m/g) from about 500 yards, then P/O Glowacki fired, after whose burst the port engine began to break up. I fired another long burst and then both engines smoked heavily, and the He.111 went down and crashed into the sea.

S/Ldr Jan Zumbach, No. 303 Sqn, 16.30

When over our ships I spotted two He.111's - I ordered the port section of four to go after one and with F/Sgt.Giermer went in to attack the other. When approaching the e/a a Spitfire from 317 Sqdn. joined us. I fired my first burst from cannons only from a distance of about 400 yds. The He.111 slowed down and I had to break away, my place being taken by the pilot from 317 Sqdn.for a while. I got in another burst and finally F/Sgt.Giermer. attacked the e/a until it crashed into the sea.

F/Sgt Wacław Giermer, No. 303 Sqn, 16.30

After arriving over the convoy and making a turn I noticed A/A fire from our ships which was directed at two He.111's. The port section of our squadron was detailed to attack the lower e/a and S/L Zumbach and I went in to attack the higher one. My leader attacked first from starboard and I went in from port and saw it had broken away the e/a dived and was followed by Sgt. Sztramko (317 Sqdn) who fired a short burst and climbed away. The two Spitfires approached 8 Fw.190's which had appeared above and following the He.111 I fired until it crashed into the sea, whereupon, I climbed away.

Sgt Kazimierz Sztramko, No. 317 Sqn, 16.30

When I heard by R/T that E/A were bombing the convoy I was to starboard of the convoy. The Squadron was ordered to turn to Port. I continued my course to bring myself to a position on the right wing of the Squadron, but meanwhile the Squadron dispersed in pursuit of E/A. I saw a He. 111 about 2,000 above me and Spitfires attacking it I therefore decided not to attack this E/A. Another He. 111 crossed the course of the convoy about the centre from E. to W. at my own level. I gave full boost and followed him but the He. 111 saw me and tried to escape by diving. I saw two more Spitfires dive towards the He. 111 from port and between it and me. I saw the leading Spitfire open fire I could not fire because these Spitfires were in the way. I turned to starboard to make a beam attack, the first Spitfire turned away to port and I fired a long burst at the He. 111 from 200-250 yds. Then I was warned by R/t that E/A were on my tail and saw tracer bullets go past. I turned and saw that they had been fired at the He. 111 by another Spitfire. Then I saw the He. 111 hit the sea.

F/Lt Kazimierz Rutkowski, No. 317 Sqn, 16.30

When our Squadron was over the Convoy I kept the Squadron in a favourable position behind the other Squadron's. After one orbit we noticed heavy A/A fire from our destroyers. Then Sgt. Kolosynski drew my attention to enemy bombers who were over the Convoy to the left. As Commander of the Squadron I gave the order for a left turn so as to get behind the bombers. The Squadron dispersed and everyone was attacking on his own. I started chasing a Do. 217 but seeing some other Spitfires catching up with it quicker than I did I turned to look for somebody else and then noticed a He. 111 who had just come out of the clouds.
At first when he saw me he tried to escape into the clouds but abandoned it and started diving towards France. I dived after him and gave him a few short bursts from long range about 400 yds. then when at 200 yds. I gave him another long burst and saw his airframe catch fire. I gave him my last burst at less than 150 yds. and then all my cannon ammunition was finished. I was warned by Sgt. Kirchner that several Fw 190 were diving after me. I turned to the left and at that moment saw my He. 111 dive into the sea. I then turned right and saw streaks in the sea where my He. 111 had dived into it. Three more Fw started chasing me and I had to do my best to get away by a series of sharp turns, but could not fire because the E/A were behind me.

F/O Stanisław Łukaszewicz, No. 317 Sqn, 16.30

When our Squadron was over the Convoy I heard by R/T that enemy bombers were to the left near the Convoy. Then I saw scattered enemy bombers and groups of Spitfires attacking them. I began to chase the nearest but abandoned it because the pursuing Spitfires were much nearer the E/A than I was. Then I saw a Heinkel III descending from the clouds and diving on the convoy pursued by a Spitfire which was followed by 4 FW. 190. I therefore left the Heinkel 111 alone and attacked the nearest of the FW. from astern. I gave full burst and from 200-250 yds. I gave him a long burst of cannon, and saw the FW. dive towards the sea out of control. My No. 2 Sgt. Praczak saw the pilot bale out this is confirmed by S/Ldr. Skalski and P/O Maciejowski.

P/O Stanisław Brzeski, No. 317 Sqn, 16.30

When with the squadron over rear end of convoy, I noticed A/A fire from our destroyers and three enemy bombers coming out of the clouds and escaping to the south.
I gave full boost and started chasing the a/c which was nearest to me, but when I saw three other Spitfires attacking this machine, I turned after a fourth bomber which I then noticed diving at sea level about 2 miles s. of the convoy. I recognised the machine to be He.111. I attacked him from astern at a range of 200-100 yards, giving him two long bursts with my cannon, until all my ammunition was finished. During my firing I saw him explode and break up. Then I saw him crash into the sea after I had fired a long burst with my machine guns. He broke up completly one mile south of the French coast.
When circling over my He.111 in the sea, I noticed about 7 Fw.190 at a distance of 3 miles to the south flying towards the convoy. I joined 2 Spitfires flying in my direction and with them joined the other Spitfires over the convoy. After a few minutes, I saw 4 Fw.190's at 2,000 feet over me, coming out of the clouds in line astern. The first one of these Fw.190's was attacked by a Spitfire. I saw the Fw.190 being hit. At that moment the next Fw.190 attacked the Spitfire. This Spitfire was hit and crashed into the sea. The pilot did not save himself.
I managed to give another Fw.190 a burst with a view of driving him off, at a range of 600 yards, but could not see the result.

P/O Michał Maciejowski, No. 317 Sqn, 16.30

After having orbited once I noticed A/A fire I saw a Do 217 escaping towards France My no 2 noticed him at the same time but being in a more favourable position caught up first with him and gave him a long burst. I followed my No 2 and when he pulled up I started chasing the Do 217 and when at a range of 30-50 yds gave him a full and long burst with my machine guns, and cannon.
The Do 217 caught fire and dived steeply into the sea. They crashed into the sea and none of the crew managed to save themselves.

Sgt Adam Kolczyński, No. 317 Sqn, 16.30

When I saw A/A fire from one of our destroyers I warned the Squadron by R/T that E/A were to port near the convoy. Immediately afterwards I saw a Do. 217 coming out of the clouds and flying S.E. I led the attack opening fire at 250-200 yds. I then attacked from astern and his rear gunner opened fire on me. I closed in and fired several long machine gun bursts which silenced the rear gunner. I fired all my remaining canon ammunition and saw the port engine of the Do. 217 smoking. Tracer bullets from astern came past me and fearing an attack from astern I turned to starboard and saw that the tracer had been fired at the Do. 217 by a Spitfire behind me. I then turned again to port and heard by R/T that the Do. 217 had hit the sea. I looked down and saw a streak on the sea.

Postscript

Ironically, when the time came for the real invasion of France in June 1944, No. 303 Squadron was again a 'resting' back-up unit and in this role it was using Spitfire Vs, by then quite obsolescent. Once more, it moved to the south of England to take part in the operation, but this time for more than just a few days. It became part of No. 142 Wing, led by W/Cdr John Checketts (see PW29 for more details).

On D-Day, the squadron had five pilots who had participated in 'Jubilee': S/Ldr Tadeusz Koc, commanding No. 303, F/Lts Brunon Kudrewicz and Józef Stasik, commanding 'A' and 'B' Flight, respectively, W/Os Aleksander Rokitnicki and Władysław Sznapka. It is worth noting that only Stasik and Rokitnicki had flown with No. 303 Sqn in August 1942, while the other three had been pilots of No. 308 Sqn at the time. During June 1944 No. 303 Sqn was joined by three more 'Jubilee' veterans, F/Lt Mirosław Szelestowski, and W/Os Ryszard Górecki and Marcin Machowiak.

Unlike in 'Jubilee', when No. 303 was the top-scoring Allied squadron, the unit's pilots failed to score during the Normandy campaign. The main concern at the time was not the enemy in the air or on the ground, but the poor condition of the obsolete aircraft, and particularly of their worn out engines. W3373 RF-U and AA860 RF-R, shown overleaf, were representative of the age of No. 303 Sqn aircraft, both built in 1941 and converted to LF.V in 1943. The unit had to soldier on with such worn out Mk Vs until it converted to Spitfire IXs in July 1944.

[307]: Horne Advanced Landing Ground (ALG) in June 1944. Left to right: F/Lt Eugeniusz Szaposznikow, W/Cdr John Checketts (No. 142 Wing Leader), G/Cpt Jerzy Bajan (Senior Polish Liaison Officer to HQ Air Defence of Great Britain), F/Lt Józef Stasik ('B' Flight Commander in No. 303 Sqn), F/Lt Brunon Kudrewicz ('A' Flight Commander) and S/Ldr Tadeusz Koc (commanding No. 303). G/Cpt Bajan flew repeatedly with No. 303 Sqn over Normandy in June 1944, two of his operational sorties were flown in W3373/RF-U, two more in AA860/RF-R. F/Lt Stasik also completed two sorties in W3373/RF-U during the invasion.

[308]: Before delivery to No. 303 Squadron in March 1944, Spitfire VB W3373 had seen service with two other Polish units. Delivered to No. 315 Sqn at Woodvale in the last days of July 1942 and coded PK-A, it was used by the unit until the beginning of September. Subsequently, it was transferred (along with all other Spitfires of No. 315) to No. 317 Squadron that replaced it there. Coded JH-A, it became the personal mount of the 'A' Flight Commander, F/Lt Marian Trzebiński. This souvenir photo, taken in late 1942, shows it as backdrop to, right to left: Cpl Edward Ancuta, Cpl Stefan Kalisz-Kalisiak, F/O Ludwik Martel, unrecognised Polish airman, unrecognised visiting US soldier (presumably of Polish descent), LAC Zdzisław Dyrka, unrecognised.

[309]: Sgt Antoni Zwierowski posing on W3373 in the spring of 1943. While in No. 317 Sqn service, the Spitfire was adorned with the name 'Ewunia', similar to other personal aircraft of Marian Trzebiński.

[310]: Spitfire VB W3373 (RF-)U, No. 303 Squadron, Horne, June 1944. Upper surface camouflage: Ocean Grey and Dark Green ('A' pattern); under surface colour: Medium Sea Grey. Polish squares both sides of the nose, with 'POLAND' stencil underneath. No. 303 Sqn badge below the windscreen on both sides of the fuselage. Special markings in form of white and black bands on the rear fuselage and wings (partly obliterating the code letters).

[311]: Two No. 303 Squadron Spitfire LF.VBs, W3373 U and AA860 R, at Horne ALG in June 1944. The Spitfires are in full invasion markings, with the squadron code obliterated completely on the fuselage. Both aircraft feature late style exhausts, typical for LF.V conversions. Notably, W3373 has clipped wings and unmodified tail surfaces, while AA860 seems to have normal elliptic tips and the later horizontal tail with enlarged horn balance on the elevator. Standing in the foreground are F/Sgt Zbigniew Bezwukto (left) and probably F/Sgt Jan Wierchowicz. Bezwukto flew two sorties in W3373 on D-Day.